RESEARCH

TO THE POINT

▼

RESEARCH

TO THE POINT

Allan A. Metcalf

<small>MacMurray College</small>

Harcourt Brace Jovanovich, Publishers

San Diego   New York   Chicago   Austin   Washington, D.C.
London   Sydney   Tokyo   Toronto

To David, Stephen, Michael, and Sara

Now you know

PREFACE

A research paper is an investigation of an idea—a hypothesis or a point about a topic. It is not an exercise in quotation, although it will use paraphrase, summary, and perhaps some quotation to support its point. Nor is it an exercise in documentation, although it must clearly and succinctly inform the reader of each source it paraphrases, summarizes, or quotes. Instead, a research paper is an exercise in thinking. It begins with a generally accepted (or perhaps generally rejected) opinion; then it develops that opinion into a well-founded judgment, possibly quite different from the original idea.

The procedures can be complex, but this simple principle gives direction and focus to every stage of the research paper. *Research to the Point* emphasizes the goal of research, not the details. Thus it enables the student to grasp the details as he or she undergoes the investigative journey that leads logically to the goal.

Too easily the student's attention is focused exclusively on academic etiquette: the form of a textual citation or bibliographic listing, punctuation, capitalization, abbreviation, spacing, margins. This textbook avoids that frustration by concentrating not on details but on an organizing principle that makes sense of the details. Thus, by showing the student how to move beyond the initial topic to a hypothesis about that topic, *Research to the Point* ensures that details will be seen as a means of supporting and clarifying the point, resulting in research that is both effective and efficient.

Research to the Point attains efficiency by showing the student how to move from topic to hypothesis even before the start of research. True, it is easier to start with a topic. But postponing the choice of hypothesis often forces the student to waste valuable time pursuing irrelevant material and fruitlessly citing one source after another in the hope that numerous citations will somehow add up to a coherent message. In fact, without a hypothesis the student cannot know what is valuable and what is not.

Beginning with a hypothesis is not as hard as it might seem. Just as topics come readily to mind, so do ideas, hunches, and opinions about those topics that can be phrased as hypotheses. And since hypotheses (as opposed to final thesis statements) do not have to be true, *Research to the Point* explores the ways in which early propositions can be tested and modified as necessary by subsequent research.

A hypothesis is simply a testable statement about a topic. It can be as simple as the answer to the question, *What do you think about this topic?* For example:

Topic: The ozone layer. *What about it?* The ozone layer is being depleted.

Topic: Democracy. *What about it?* Democracies do not start wars.

To require proof of a hypothesis would be impossible at the beginning; the whole point of research is to inquire about its validity. But an idea is a strong beginning for a research paper.

Every activity in *Research to the Point* assists the student's efficient progress from hypothesis to finished research paper. For example, three early chapters are devoted to helping the student develop an effective hypothesis. Part I closes with the assignment of a 500-word research proposal, ensuring that the student will think carefully about the hypothesis before starting research. The next step, likewise requiring thoughtfulness and aimed at efficiency, is to search *Library of Congress Subject Headings* for key words. Then comes an opportunity to gain an overview of the subject matter from encyclopedias and other works in the library's reference collection. The student is then fully prepared for the chief work of a research paper: finding, citing, listing, and writing about sources. Part V explains how the final paper begins with a thesis derived from the hypothesis and supports the thesis with evidence from the sources.

The lesson of each stage is summarized in the Introduction as well as in the chapter headings. Therefore, the student who has finished a stage or mastered a principle may go directly to the next activity, aided by numerous cross references.

The textbook gives special emphasis to the fundamental skill of properly using a source: determining what material is relevant to the hypothesis, then writing an explanation of its relevance. This means writing statements that support, clarify, qualify, or challenge the hypothesis. These statements later can be incorporated into the body of the paper. There is no room for unexplained paraphrase and quotation. The student remains in charge of the material, rather than vice versa.

At all stages the student is encouraged to rethink the hypothesis to determine unambiguously what material is relevant and what is not. As new evidence appears, the student will adapt the hypothesis to fit that evidence more precisely.

Although the book does not focus on formalities, it does not slight them. With documentation, as elsewhere, *Research to the Point* aims to empower the student by teaching basic principles rather than presenting endless details. Students are taught to cite and list sources according to the principles of Modern Language Association style. For added simplification, MLA style has been distilled into three basic forms for the list of Works

Cited, rather than many rules and a long, inevitably incomplete list of examples. For any source, the student chooses from just three examples that can be extended to fit nearly all cases. For those who wish more detail, Chapter 11 gives instructions on MLA abbreviation and documentation for special cases. The "basic MLA" can easily be converted to the full professional version when the student is ready to write papers for publication. The alternative style of the American Psychological Association is explained in Appendix III.

Completeness and accuracy should be the uppermost concerns in documentation. A mistake in style is correctable; an error in naming a source is not. Hence *Research to the Point* instructs the student to provide a photocopy of each page used as a source, so that student and instructor can check accuracy of citation.

Among the incidental benefits of this book's approach to the research paper is that it allows students to work on the same topic without duplication when each has a different hypothesis. Its step-by-step assignments and required photocopies also make plagiarism difficult.

Research has an important function in the direction of our world and an impact on all of us. *Research to the Point* aims to train students to be real participants in this research, not mere imitators.

Acknowledgments

For four years faculty members in English and other departments at MacMurray College have put this book to the test. Their advice, questions, and complaints about earlier versions have vastly improved the usefulness of the present work. My heartfelt thanks therefore go to these colleagues: Professors Mary Anthony, Ray Bugayong, Larry Calhoun, Donna Chenoweth, John Church, Elizabeth Crowley, Guy Crumley, Jonathan Dixon, Jim Goulding, Richard Hanson, Edwin Hockett, J. Michael Jones, Mickey Jones, Margret Kerbaugh, Jan Kvale, Richard McGuire, Penny Mitchell, Jay Peterson, Robert Seufert, Kathleen Sigle, Anita Sorrill, Frances Suess, and Margaret Wilson.

I owe particular thanks also to William J. Kerrigan, who first taught the importance of writing to the point; to Stephen Metcalf, who first experimented with my instructions; to Scott Hester, who printed the first trial version as fast as it was ready, and to Richard Marshall, who arranged for subsequent printings; to Penny Mitchell at the MacMurray College Library for her advice on reference sources and documentation, and to Martin Gallas, Pat Schildman, and Roger Swartzbaugh at the Illinois College library; to Philip Decker for valuable suggestions; and above all, to the students who tested earlier versions of this book over the past four years. Among those who were especially helpful I must name Suszan Cadwell, Eric Carter, Frank Peppers, and Carol Schwalb. And I appreciate Jamie Eshbaugh's willingness to have her papers serve as models for others.

I also appreciate the encouragement and prodding of Professors Robert H. Bentley of Lansing Community College and Mary Alea of the University of Wisconsin, Eau Claire. At Harcourt Brace Jovanovich this book was made possible by editors Paul Nockleby and Stuart Miller, manuscript editor Karen Carriere, production editor Kristina Sanfilippo, designer James Hughes, and production manager David Hough. My sincere thanks to them all.

Allan Metcalf

CONTENTS

▽

PART IV: WRITING ABOUT SOURCES

PART V: THE FINAL PAPER

APPENDIXES

Introduction

▽

CHAPTER ONE

THE POINT OF RESEARCH

▽

A research paper centers on a hypothesis which develops into the thesis of the paper after being tested against evidence found in research sources.

(The rest of this book offers detailed explanations: on the hypothesis, Chapters 2, 3, and 4; on finding sources of evidence, Chapters 5 through 8; on listing and citing sources, Chapters 9 through 11; on writing about sources, Chapters 12 through 16; on the final thesis and paper, Chapters 17 through 19.)

▽

Research is the heart of education and the engine of progress.

When you undertake research, you undertake real work of the mind. Research is the work of scholars who look for literary influences on an author or the origins of a political movement; of scientists who look for the means by which stars are formed or a disease may be cured. Research is the work of journalists investigating a story, lawyers preparing for a case, investors looking to buy stocks, consumers shopping for cars. In fact, we all do research when, instead of simply taking someone's word for it, we investigate a proposition ourselves, find out the facts of the situation, consider the views of various experts, and then make up our own minds.

So a research paper is not an idle exercise but an activity that should engage your mind to the fullest. Instead of simply repeating something your instructor has told you, you will learn a lesson on your own and possibly teach the instructor something she or he did not know.

Because it requires both research and documentation (citing and listing sources), a research paper is a more challenging assignment than a personal essay or statement of opinion. But it is not something totally different; it is just more complex. You do not abandon your own ideas and views when you write a research paper. The difference is that you support those views with the evidence you find in your research.

A research paper is personal opinion augmented by the facts, by insights from others. This is the opinion we respect, the opinion that persuades us. We are not ready to agree that

▼ Generic drugs are as safe as brand-name ones.

merely on the basis of one experience with a doctor's prescription, but we will pay attention to someone who supports that proposition with evidence from scientific studies and the reports of government agencies.

Likewise, we are properly skeptical of someone who merely states a hunch that

▼ Mary Shelley's novel *Frankenstein* reflects modern attitudes towards science.

But we are ready to agree with that opinion if someone supports it with evidence concerning modern attitudes toward science—and evidence concerning what Mary Shelley wrote.

Evidence is required to persuade us that

▼ T.S. Eliot was an influence on literary deconstruction theory

—if he was—or that

▼ The opening of the Berlin Wall showed the failure of Communism.

Providing the evidence is the work of the research paper. The research paper, in fact, is the process of turning a hunch, an initial opinion, into a thesis supported by evidence.

The complexity of the research paper assignment, and the need to look for what others have found and said, can cause difficulties. Later chapters will address these. But at the beginning the most serious hazard of all is the danger of wasting time, and it is such a temptation because yielding to it is so much easier than getting down to the serious business of research and writing to the point. You can waste time by:

• Waiting to choose a topic.

• Waiting to make a point—a hypothesis—about the topic.

• Reading and taking notes on material unrelated to your hypothesis.

The more background reading you do, the better. The more you know about your topic and about the world, the better. But unless you have unlimited time, you must make your research as efficient as possible, for it will still take as much time as you can spare.

Another danger for the writer of a research paper is a mistaken idea of its purpose. It is all too easy to concentrate on the outward appearance of the research paper: title, margins, indentations, punctuation and capitalization, and especially the formal details of bibliography listings. These details are necessary, and we will take some time explaining them. The purpose of a research paper, however, is not to look nice but to say something—just as the purpose of a symphony orchestra is not to wear formal evening clothes but to make music, and the purpose of a baseball team is not to wear uniforms but to play ball.

The formal details of a research paper have always required attention, sometimes to the extent of distracting students from having anything to say. Fortunately, recent developments have made it possible to attend to formalities more efficiently. One development is a simpler form for referring to sources. Instead of requiring footnotes plus bibliography, a research paper nowadays requires only a bibliography—a list of Works Cited—with simple citations in the text referring the reader to that list.

Another development is the availability of the copying machine, which makes it possible to have copies of your sources at hand during all stages of the research process and to mark passages and make marginal notes on the copies. This makes greater accuracy possible and permits you to return to a source for something you may have overlooked at first.

A third development is increasing use of the computer, both for bibliographic searches and for word processing. Computer searching of bibliographic references, available at many libraries, is much speedier than looking through printed reference volumes. Nor is it just a matter of speed; computer databases allow you to narrow your search while using combinations of broad headings that would take too long to search by hand. The ability to combine key words permits the use of broad terms such as "Safety" with "Generic drugs," for example, "Science" with *"Frankenstein,"* or "Communism" with "Berlin Wall." (Chapter 8 discusses these possibilities.)

Furthermore, if one is available to you, a word-processing program in a computer can put the text of your paper and your list of Works Cited in the right format, fit your corrections instantly into your text, and even check your style, punctuation, and spelling.

But whether you work with a computer or pen and paper, the chief work of a research paper remains the same. It is not a matter of format but of thinking—and then looking at the thinking of others to see how well it agrees with yours. If you focus your thoughts from the beginning on a research hypothesis and keep them on that point, you will waste the least time and make the most sense.

Efficient, successful research requires the use of your judgment at every stage. You will understand the necessary attitude if you imagine yourself involved in a courtroom trial. A trial always tests a proposition, a hypothesis: that someone (or something) does or did something. Lawyers bring evidence, and witnesses offer testimony, for and against this hypothesis. The judge considers the evidence, decides for or against the hypothesis, and then writes an opinion, using the evidence to support that decision. When you write a research paper, you are the judge.

In fact, for a research paper you also have to take the part of the lawyers on both sides. You find the evidence and the witnesses and arrange for their testimony. But above all, you are the judge. As a good judge, you will consider all sides of the question. You will also rule digressions out of order and will determine the case as efficiently as possible. Your time is too valuable to waste.

This book is designed to help you reach that informed judgment. It instructs you in the necessary details of form and procedure, but it emphasizes principles. You can never learn all the rules, but you can learn the principles behind them, and then you can always render a fair decision without becoming entangled in technicalities.

Each chapter deals with a single stage in the process of writing a research paper. The chapters come in a logical progression, but they are arranged so that you may take them in a different order if your research assignment calls for it. The lesson of each chapter is summarized at its beginning. If you already know the lesson, or if you are not yet ready for it, you can follow the references to other chapters for the information you need.

Whatever the particular order of lessons, the basic procedure remains the same. To be as effective and efficient as you need to be, you must *begin with a hypothesis,* a proposition, a point about a topic. Next, you will *look for sources of relevant evidence*—evidence to support, oppose, or modify the original hypothesis. You will *write explanations* of the evidence these sources provide and will *cite and list the sources,* telling who wrote them and where they were published. You will arrange these explanations in the body of the research paper after *a final thesis,* which is the hypothesis modified as necessary to accord with the evidence.

That, in brief, is the whole activity of writing a research paper. It is as simple, and as difficult, as that.

The rest of this book is divided into five parts, taking you step by step through the five principal stages:

- hypothesis
- finding sources
- listing and citing sources
- writing about sources
- final thesis and paper.

It is important to note that the three middle stages dealing with sources are connected and recursive. That is, you go through them again and again for each source: finding it, listing and citing it, and writing about it. When sufficient sources are at hand, the last stage is writing the paper: converting the hypothesis into a final thesis and presenting the evidence that relates to it.

This book is an entire course in the research paper—if you have the time. But if time is limited, or if you are using this book on your own, you may instead look at this as a reference work, turning as needed to the chapters that answer your questions and illustrate the principles. However you use the book, what remains essential is to keep a steady focus on the hypothesis, the point you are testing, as it develops from an initial idea into the final thesis.

Here, in summary, are the five stages of research.

PART I: HYPOTHESIS

Before beginning research, form a hypothesis—a sentence that makes a point to be tested, a statement about a topic. A topic alone will not suffice.

Example of a topic: The greenhouse effect

Example of hypothesis using that topic: The greenhouse effect has warmed the earth in the past century.

Example of a topic: Jane Austen's novels

Example of hypothesis using that topic: Jane Austen's novels have only one plot.

Example of a topic: Perestroika

Example of hypothesis using that topic: Perestroika has not improved the economy of the Soviet Union.

Example of a topic: Confidential adoption

Example of hypothesis using that topic: Confidential adoption is better for the child's mental health than open adoption.

The hypothesis anticipates the judgment you will reach after your research. It does *not* have to be correct; you will know its correctness only after you have tested it. But it does have to be testable. You must be able to find evidence for or against it.

A hypothesis does require a topic, of course, and it may be necessary to spend a while becoming acquainted with a topic before proposing a research hypothesis. But the effort of research cannot be efficient, or even relevant, until you have a hypothesis.

Chapter 2 explains and illustrates this important first step. Chapter 3 offers advice on creating a hypothesis: consider what you know and what you read, and ask questions. Chapter 4 presents criteria for checking the hypothesis to make sure it is suitable for research and also calls for a 500-word research proposal based on the hypothesis. The proposal can serve as an outline for subsequent research and writing.

PART II: FINDING SOURCES

Find sources of information to support, oppose, or modify the hypothesis. Consult indexes, bibliographies, catalogs, and computer databases to locate sources of sufficient quantity, variety, timeliness, and quality.

Even a modest-sized college or public library has an astonishing amount of information on a vast variety of subjects, and all are able to obtain much more through interlibrary loan. The problem is that of the needle in the haystack: finding those items which speak directly not just to your topic but to your hypothesis.

To do this you will need to find appropriate key words to use while searching in indexes and bibliographies. Your best guide to key words is the *Library of Congress Subject Headings;* Chapter 5 explains its use.

General encyclopedias and other reference works can give you an overview of the subject matter of your hypothesis. Chapter 6 introduces these works and also the methods of writing about sources that will be explained more fully in later chapters.

In the library's reference collection you will find the indexes and bibliographies that, along with the book catalog, will direct you to the in-depth sources you will need for your paper. Chapter 7 focuses on this central activity of research: finding sources that are of sufficient quantity, variety, timeliness, and quality. Chapter 8 explains the added efficiency of bibliographic searches by computer.

PART III: LISTING AND CITING

For each source you use, list full publication information in a list of Works Cited. In the text of your paper, cite the author and state the page each time you use a source.

When you use a source, you must *cite* and *list* it. You name its author in your text and then provide sufficient additional information in a list of Works Cited so that your reader can locate a copy of the same source in any library that has it.

The in-text citation and list of Works Cited taught here follow the widely-used style established by the Modern Language Association of America for scholarly articles. Chapter 9 introduces the essence of listing works, MLA style, with three basic forms which can adapt to almost all kinds of sources. For a *book*, needed information includes the author, title, edition, publishing company, and year of publication; for an *article in a book*, author, title, editor, and pages, as well as edition, publishing company, and year of publication;

for an *article in a periodical*, author, title, name of the periodical, volume number, exact date of issue, pages. Chapter 9 shows not only how to display this information, but where to find it, something that is sometimes far from obvious.

Chapter 10 explains the practice of citing author and page in the text of your paper every time you use information from a source.

Special cases and further specifics of MLA style are given in Chapter 11. Other fields have their own rules for documentation, but once you have learned the principles underlying MLA style, you will be able to adapt to a different form if your instructor requires it of you. Chapter 11 and Appendix III describe one widely-used alternative: the author-year (APA) style common to the social sciences.

It is important to realize that listing and citing are done not for their own sake but for the purpose of communicating clearly and efficiently the results of research. In a larger sense, it is important to realize that this is the function of the research paper itself. Its goal is not to parade sources but to communicate the understanding gained from reviewing the sources. The details of form are a means to an end.

PART IV: WRITING ABOUT SOURCES

For each source, write an explanation of the evidence it provides to support, oppose, or modify the hypothesis.

This is the heart of research. It is not enough to copy material from a source; you must explain it. Use your own words, paraphrasing or summarizing material from a source, to explain how a source provides evidence for or against the hypothesis. Part IV, Chapters 12–16, shows this principle in operation.

The temptation to quote, to use the exact words of the source, should generally be resisted. A research paper is not a collection of quotations but your own analysis of a proposition, explained in your own words. The sources you use are written for their own purposes; they do not speak directly to your hypothesis, because they do not know what it is. On the other hand, there will be times when the words of the source say exactly what you would like to say. For those occasions, Chapter 14 provides guidelines and examples.

Whether you use your own words or those of the source, you must always cite a source each time you use it and include it in the list of Works Cited. It will be emphasized that you *cite and list the source, even if you do not quote from it, even if you put the material of the source entirely in your own words; you must always cite the cource.*

PART V: THE FINAL PAPER

Convert your hypothesis to a thesis statement, limiting and adjusting it as necessary to fit the evidence provided by the sources. Begin the paper with this thesis; follow it with the supporting evidence, and end by replying to objections.

The hypothesis, suitably modified, becomes the *thesis statement* of the final research paper. Chapter 17 explains this concluding principle.

Having a thesis as focus solves the problem of what you should put in the body of your research paper. It consists of your explanations of how the source material supports the thesis, material you developed in Part IV.

Of course, not all of the evidence provided by your sources will necessarily favor your final thesis. There is often much to be said on both sides. You, the judge, will make your decision; but you, the fair judge, will grant the strength of opposing views, explaining either how the opposing views are mistaken or how, though true, they do not outweigh the evidence on the side you have chosen.

The research paper typically begins with the thesis, presents the evidence supporting it, then considers opposing views and replies to them. An outline helps organize your presentation of the evidence, and an abstract summarizes the paper. Those are explained in Chapter 18. Lastly, Chapter 19 shows the final form.

The five appendixes summarize instructions, offer worksheets, and explain the author-date APA style.

As this introductory chapter illustrates, the process of writing a research paper involves several stages and numerous steps. There are countless details to attend to. There are also numerous distractions in the library. Fascinating books and articles about everything under the sun can make it all too easy to drift without getting anywhere.

But this book offers protection from that danger: a point, a statement about a topic. Focusing on this point will keep your source material relevant and will keep you in charge. The basic instruction of this book can be summarized as follows: *Begin with a hypothesis and keep your attention on it until you have turned it into the final thesis of your research paper.* The next three chapters explain the start of this process: the choice of a hypothesis.

▽

PART I

Hypothesis

▽

CHAPTER TWO

THE STARTING POINT

▽

Before beginning research, form a hypothesis—a sentence that makes a point to be tested, a statement about a topic. A topic alone will not suffice.

(On finding a hypothesis, see Chapter 3. On testing the hypothesis before you begin research, see Chapter 4.)

▽

The beginning of research is not a topic but an idea. We will call the idea with which the research process begins by its proper name: the research hypothesis.

A hypothesis is a sentence that makes a point, a statement of opinion about a topic. A topic alone will not suffice.

A hypothesis, in the sense we use it here, is a theory, a tentative assumption about a situation. It is something to be tested. In the process of writing a library research paper, you first form a hypothesis and then look for articles and books that provide evidence regarding the hypothesis— evidence that it is true, or that its opposite is true, or that a modified version of it is true.

Notice that the hypothesis is the very beginning of the research process. That is, the first thing you do in preparing to write a research paper is propose a hypothesis. You do this before you undertake any research. You do not even need to set foot in the library.

Let us see what happens when we put this principle in practice.

Here are a few examples, first of topics—which are not enough—and then of hypotheses about the topics.

Topic: Dreams
Hypothesis using that topic: Dreams are essential for mental health.

Topic: Athletic training
Hypothesis using that topic: Athletic training improves body responses.

Topic: Lasers
Hypothesis using that topic: Lasers are beneficial in surgery.

Topic: The stock market
Hypothesis using that topic: The stock market is a leading indicator of trends in the economy.

Topic: Nuclear power plants
Hypothesis using that topic: Nuclear power plants are safe.

Topic: Positive reinforcement
Hypothesis using that topic: Positive reinforcement is the most effective form of discipline.

Topic: Equal wages for men and women
Hypothesis using that topic: Women do not earn as much as men for comparable work.

Topic: Mark Twain
Hypothesis using that topic: Mark Twain was a radical social critic.

Topic: Apartheid in South Africa
Hypothesis using that topic: Apartheid causes hardship for all races in South Africa.

Topic: Television watching by teenagers
Hypothesis using that topic: Television watching weakens the academic performance of high school students.

In each of these cases, the topic by itself is not enough. The research paper must begin with a hypothesis, a full sentence that says what the topic is or was, does or did.

Every topic, of course, allows many different hypotheses. With "television watching by teenagers," for example, instead of the hypothesis mentioned above, you could write:

▼ Television watching improves the academic performance of high school students.

▼ Television watching does not affect the academic performance of high school students.

▼ Teenagers are the largest audience for television rock videos.

▼ Advertisers of stereo equipment target teenage television viewers.

▼ Television watching declines during the later teen years.

And there are many more possibilities.

The different possible hypotheses that stem from a single topic need not agree. Indeed, one can be the opposite of another. That is to be expected. At this early stage, your hypothesis is not a statement based on fact but an opinion still to be tested. As you test the hypothesis with your research, you may well find yourself needing to modify it. In fact, you may even need to restate it as the opposite of the original. If so, fine. You have to face the facts and be honest, just as you in turn will persuade your reader by presenting the reader with the facts.

But still you begin with a hypothesis. This way, every step of your research will have a point. And you will know exactly what to look for—namely, evidence that supports, opposes, or modifies the hypothesis. Anything else is irrelevant.

For example, if your hypothesis is

▼ Television viewing lowers the academic performance of high school students.

you need not look at articles about the commercials teenagers watch or the number of television sets teenagers own. You will look only for sources that *combine* the topics "television viewing by teenagers" and "academic performance."

In the early stages of research it is typical to find a large number of articles and books on a topic like "television viewing by teenagers." The inefficient researcher reads them all, looking for something to say. The efficient researcher skims each article and looks in the *index* of each book for material specifically relating to the point about the topic—to the "academic performance of teenagers," in this case.

To take another example, if your hypothesis is

▼ Dreams are essential for mental health.

you won't bother with articles about whether dreams can prophesy the future.

Does this principle sound familiar? It should, for it is one we use whenever we are thinking. We do our thinking and our speaking, usually, not in topics but in sentences, and that is what a hypothesis turns out to be: a sentence, a declarative sentence, the most common kind. It applies to everyday topics—even something as simple as lunch. If you start thinking about lunch, it won't stay a topic long but will turn into a hypothesis:

Topic: Lunch

Hypotheses on that topic: Lunch is whatever I find in the refrigerator. The Landmark Cafe is a good place for lunch.

Or you may be thinking about a place or a person.

Topic: The library

Hypotheses on that topic: The library has 200 books for every student. The library has a special collection of books about the English diarist Samuel Pepys. The library is a good place to meet people.

Topic: A friend

Hypotheses on that topic: Sara asks lots of questions. Steve's letter was hilarious. Mike goes jogging every morning.

We use hypotheses for the most intimate and important moments of our life:

Topics: Me, you

Hypotheses on those topics: I'm hungry. I love you.

Obviously, such statements are not suitable for library research. (Chapter 4 will offer a number of tests for the suitability of possible hypotheses). But like true research hypotheses, all these thoughts and concerns are in the form of sentences, complete statements instead of mere topics. When our minds are at work, we may start with topics, but we don't stop there. We go on to make statements out of topics, using a topic typically as the subject of a declarative sentence:

The topic) (is or was something.

The topic) (does or did something.

Topic: Microcomputers

Statement about that topic: Microcomputers are becoming more user-friendly.

Topic: The beaches of Maine

Statement about that topic: The finest beaches in Maine are in Reid State Park.

So you already know, from long practice, the first principle that makes research efficient and writing effective. It is present in your subconscious, ready to be called on. Just keep on using it when you approach the research paper. Keep on expressing your ideas not just in topics, but in statements about those topics.

When your work lacks this thinking—when research and writing deal only with a topic rather than making a statement about that topic—the research paper seems a pointless exercise in academic manners, notable only for the amount and variety of material that must be strung together according to an esoteric system of etiquette.

In fact, that kind of exercise is not a research paper; it is a travesty of one. Real research involves real thinking, or it would not have become the important force it now is in the real world. Journalists, scientists, advertisers, politicians, medical doctors, and lawyers—as well as spies, detectives, and librarians—conduct research by purposefully testing hypotheses that are central to the work they conduct. College professors, too, conduct research, not by browsing through the library's holdings (they do that, as you can, for recreation or to get ideas for future research), but by devising a hypothesis and testing to see if it is true. So real research will concern itself with hypotheses like these:

Topic: Air pollution

Hypothesis: Air pollution is warming the planet.

Topic: Freedom of expression

Hypothesis: Freedom of expression promotes scientific progress.

Topic: Caffeine

Hypothesis: Caffeine is addictive.

Topic: Nuclear weapons

Hypothesis: Nuclear weapons preserve the balance of peace.

Topic: The Sunbelt

Hypothesis: The Sunbelt is no longer leading the United States in economic development.

Topic: Terrorism

Hypothesis: Military retaliation stops terrorism.

Topic: Taxes

Hypothesis: Low tax rates lead to economic growth.

Topic: Prisons

Hypothesis: Prisons educate inmates to be criminals.

Topic: Patriotism

Hypothesis: "Patriotism is the last refuge of a scoundrel." (These are the words of Dr. Samuel Johnson, eighteenth-century English writer.)

Topic: The American Constitution

Hypothesis: The American Constitution has lasted two centuries because it assumes individuals will be concerned above all with their own self-interest.

The list could go on and on, indefinitely—and it does.

It should be added that at this beginning stage hypotheses are statements not of truth but of opinion. They are merely theories. Investigation may show that the opposite is true, and it is quite possible that different researchers will sift the evidence to reach different, even opposite, conclusions. Research, however, raises discussion of these matters from mere difference of opinion to acknowledgment of truths that must underlie any intelligent opinion, truths that increase the chances of arriving at enlightened judgments.

Your research thus becomes a matter of testing the hypothesis and modifying it to accord with the facts and details you discover. And your research paper then becomes an explanation of the evidence you have found that confirms and explains your suitably modified hypothesis.

Here, then, is first an exercise and then the assignment that will be the important first step on the road to a successful research paper:

EXERCISE 2.1

Think of at least one hypothesis for each of these topics. Which do you find easiest? Which do you find most difficult? Why? (See Chapter 3 for further discussion of workable hypotheses.)

1. Music
2. Life on other planets
3. Happiness
4. The "baby boom" generation
5. Sleep
6. Communism
7. The Cold War
8. Exercise
9. Microcomputers
10. Tickling
11. Bicycles
12. Revenge
13. Beauty
14. Summer vacations
15. Stephen King's novels

ASSIGNMENT I—HYPOTHESIS

Following the instructions of this chapter, write a possible hypothesis for your research paper. Make sure it is not just a topic, but a sentence that says what the topic is or was, does or did.

Your instructor may put some conditions on this assignment. At one extreme, you may be assigned a hypothesis, or given a list of ready-made hypotheses to choose from. Or you may be limited to a certain topic or range of topics. No matter how limited the topics, however, the number of possible hypotheses remains unlimited.

You may be assigned to start with a topic you find in a current magazine, newspaper, or other reading material. You may be sent to the library to browse. And you may be assigned to come up with not just one but several possible hypotheses, perhaps as many as half a dozen, so that later you will be able to choose the most promising. If you need help in thinking of hypotheses, turn to the next chapter.

Once you have your hypothesis, take some time to think about what you have written. Chapter 4 will show how to use this time to give your possible hypothesis the careful review it needs before you proceed with your research.

▽

CHAPTER THREE

FINDING A POINT

▽

To create a hypothesis, consider what you know and what you read, and ask questions.

On the need for a hypothesis, see Chapter 2. If you already have a hypothesis, examine it for suitability, as explained in Chapter 4.

▽

To begin the research process, you have to find not just a topic but a hypothesis. If your own interests and the instructions in Chapter 2 have already produced your hypothesis, well and good; you can proceed with the testing of the hypothesis in Chapter 4. If not, this chapter offers some suggestions. Determining a hypothesis is not so hard, if you do some serious thinking.

Here are some steps to take:

1. Start with what you know.

There is much in anyone's experience that suggests ideas for research hypotheses. For example, most of us grew up in families. The experience of families can give us hypotheses like these (or their opposites):

▼ Oldest children are typically the greatest achievers.

▼ Reading aloud to preschoolers influences them to become avid readers.

▼ Caring for a dog contributes to a child's mental health.

▼ Parental models influence teenage drinking behavior.

▼ Adults go through stages of development just as children do.

Another experience most of us have had is television. Thinking about television can lead to hypotheses about viewers or the medium itself. For example:

▼ Television advertising is especially effective for introducing new goods and services.

▼ Viewers who have cable switch channels more often than those who do not.

▼ Viewers understand only about one-third of network television news stories.

▼ Violence in children's television is increasing.

Do you live on a farm, in a small town, in a city or a suburb? Wherever you live, there are local issues worthy of research. You can investigate such hypotheses as:

▼ Price supports keep farmers from bankruptcy.

▼ Small towns have less crime per capita than big cities.

▼ Property taxes provide a growing share of local government revenue.

▼ Mass transportation is gaining ridership.

In addition to the experiences everyone has had, you will have distinctive ones of your own. Your jobs and hobbies and the classes you have taken can provide possibilities for hypotheses; so can your travels, your possessions, and the people you have met.

2. Start with what you read.

Browse in the library. Try the current periodicals section. Pick up a scholarly journal, a newsmagazine, a newspaper. The national newspaper *USA Today*, for example, carries arguments on both sides of a current issue every day on its editorial page. But almost any periodical will do. A recent Sunday edition of a small-town daily newspaper, for example, suggested these possible hypotheses:

▼ World oil reserves are abundant.

▼ The success of American agriculture depends on free trade with the rest of the world.

▼ Americans prefer the quality and style of foreign-made clothes.

▼ Retired Americans are financially better off than middle-aged workers.

▼ Term life insurance is more economical than whole life.

▼ Government-provided jobs are less costly than welfare payments.

▼ Lowering tax rates raises tax revenue.

▼ Seat belts save lives.

▼ Devices that monitor patients' breathing can prevent deaths from anesthesia.

▼ Imported stingless wasps are more effective than pesticides in controlling the alfalfa beetle.

▼ The three-point basketball shot reduces the advantage of the tall player.

In fact, headlines and opening paragraphs of a news story sometimes contain a ready-made hypothesis. Reports of scientific or other studies are especially useful. For example:

▼ Sewage dumped at sea poses a significant health risk to seafood lovers and swimmers.

▼ The United States trails its foreign competitors in the health and care of children.

▼ Bone-marrow transplant is the treatment of choice for certain cancers.

▼ Humor may be necessary for success at work.

▼ A well-tended garden filled with exotic plants was a sign of culture and wealth in 19th-century America.

You can also find inspiration in the reference collection. Browse in a general encyclopedia or specialized reference work in a field that interests you. Perhaps your reference collection includes the *Opposing Viewpoints* and *Opposing Viewpoints Sources* books published by Greenhaven Press. The chapter titles in each of these books are potential research hypotheses (except those with *should* or *must*—see Chapter 4). The *Opposing Viewpoints Sources* volume on *Chemical Dependency,* for example, has a hundred chapters with titles like:

• Addiction Is Epidemic
• The Drug Addiction Crisis Is Media Hype
• Alcoholism Is a Disease
• Crackdowns on Drunk Driving Are Effective
• Passive Smoking Is Harmful
• Banning Cigarette Advertising Is Constitutional
• Drug Laws Increase Crime
• The War on Drugs Is Succeeding
• Drug Testing Benefits Society

Remove the extra capital letters and put a period at the end of one of these titles, and you have a workable research hypothesis.

3. Ask a question.

You can also begin with a question, from your reading or your life, which you then go on to answer. Questions that begin with *What, Why*, and *How* are especially useful; some will also begin with *Is* or *Are, Does* or *Did*. (Again, do not use *should;* see the explanation in Chapter 4.) The provisional answer to the question is your research hypothesis. Let the phrasing of the question guide the phrasing of your hypothesis. For example:

What is the best material for the reflector of an astronomical telescope?

▼ Liquid mercury makes the best material for the reflector of an astronomical telescope.

How does a compact disc compare with a cassette tape in fidelity of sound reproduction?

▼ A compact disc is superior to a cassette tape in fidelity of sound reproduction.

What started the Crusades?

▼ The Crusades were started by the preaching of Pope Urban II at the Council of Clermont in 1095.

What is the effect of price subsidies for crops?

▼ Price subsidies encourage agricultural overproduction.

Why does Hamlet hesitate to take revenge for his murdered father?

▼ Hamlet hesitates to take revenge for his murdered father because he doubts the word of the ghost.

Who invented the calculus?

▼ Newton and Leibniz both invented the calculus independently, each incorporating features that the other did not have.

Are parents of battered children likely to have been battered children themselves?

▼ Parents of battered children are likely to have been battered children themselves.

In summary, then, to decide on a hypothesis: consider what you know; notice what you read; ask a question and give it a tentative answer. From any of these exercises at least one hypothesis should emerge. Remember that although the hypothesis needs to be a sentence (and to meet the seven conditions stated in the next chapter), it does not have to be correct; it is your best guess at the moment, but it is fully ready to be changed to fit the evidence. Improving the hypothesis as you go along is a normal part of the research process.

EXERCISE 3.1

The following questions are titles of *Opposing Viewpoints Pamphlets*. Write a possible research hypothesis for each one by answering the question, keeping as close as possible to the phrasing of the question.

1. Is U.S. Intervention the Cause of Latin America's Problems?
2. Are Latin American Revolutions a Threat to the United States?
3. How Serious Is the Latin American Debt?
4. Why Is the Middle East a Conflict Area?
5. Are Palestinian Rights Being Ignored?
6. Have the Superpowers Hindered Africa's Development?
7. Why Is Famine Prevalent in Africa?
8. How Strong Is the Soviet Economy?
9. Why Is the Third World Poor?
10. Does U.S. Foreign Aid Benefit the Third World?
11. How Do Prisons Affect Criminals?
12. What Are the Alternatives to Prison?
13. What Causes Crime?
14. Is the Litigation Crisis Destroying the Legal System?
15. Are Lawyers Ethical?
16. Is Sex Education Beneficial?
17. Do the Superpowers Sponsor Terrorism?
18. Are Humans Aggressive by Nature?
19. What Causes War?
20. Are Peace Movements Effective?

Now consider these questions from *Opposing Viewpoints Books:*
21. Is Pornography Harmful?
22. Is Free Trade Good for the Economy?
23. Is a Holistic Lifestyle Healthier?
24. How Are Sex Roles Established?
25. What Affects Teenagers' Attitudes Toward Sex?
26. Why Does Poverty Disproportionately Affect Minorities?

27. Do Women Receive Equal Treatment?
28. Are the Media Biased?
29. How Dangerous Are Toxic Wastes?
30. How Did Life Originate?

In answering these questions, do not worry if you are not sure of the answers. At this stage, in fact, a little humility is welcome. Your answer is a guess, a hunch, a *hypothesis*. The point of the research process is to test that hypothesis and modify it as appropriate until it becomes the final thesis.

List of Works Cited in Chapter 3

Opposing Viewpoints Pamphlets. San Diego, CA: Greenhaven Press, Inc., 1990.

Opposing Viewpoints Series. San Diego, CA: Greenhaven Press, Inc., 1990.

Opposing Viewpoints Sources: Chemical Dependency. San Diego, CA: Greenhaven Press, Inc., 1989.

▽

CHAPTER FOUR

THINKING ABOUT THE POINT

▽

Examine the hypothesis to see if it is suitable for research.

(On the need for a hypothesis, see Chapter 2. For help in deciding on a hypothesis, see Chapter 3. If you have a suitable hypothesis, proceed to the assignment at the end of this chapter and then to the start of research, Chapter 5.)

▽

Before you even begin your library research, some of the most important work of the research paper takes place, the work of determining what your hypothesis will be. It may seem easy enough, considering that a hypothesis amounts to no more than a single declarative sentence that states your judgment about a topic. You can write that sentence in a minute, if you are in a hurry to move on. But since this one sentence points the direction of all the research you will be doing, it deserves your full and careful attention now, to save frustration later.

For unfortunately, not any declarative sentence will do. Only certain sentences lend themselves to the challenging work of a research hypothesis: to present a proposition that can be tested by sources available to you, to guide all of your research, and then to end up, suitably modified, as the thesis—the main point—of your final research paper.

Pausing to examine your hypothesis as soon as you have decided on it may seem an unnecessary delay in the research process. In fact, however, you can make a judgment as to the suitability of a hypothesis even before you undertake any research. Doing so, you will avoid wasting research time on an unworkable hypothesis.

Do not be surprised if your initial hypothesis turns out to be not entirely suitable. An initial idea may well need some rethinking. But you need not abandon a topic you want to investigate, provided you are willing to set aside an unsuitable hypothesis on that topic and find one that is more appropriate. No topic, by itself, will automatically work for a research paper, just as no topic is automatically excluded. It all depends on the hypothesis you form.

NINE CONDITIONS

We can identify nine major conditions for an effective research hypothesis. The first is this:

1. Write a statement that requires testing.

Statements such as the following are not suitable for research, simply because no research is needed to establish them as true or false.

The sun is shining today.

The library is open from 2 to 9 p.m. on Sundays.

I like broccoli.

It is easy to see why these sentences will not work. "The sun is shining today" tells an obvious fact, if it is true, or an obvious lie, if it is not true. In either case, that statement calls for no more research than walking to the nearest window and looking out. Other statements about weather, of course, can be hypotheses for research, such as

▼ Pollution is causing summers to be hotter.

The second hypothesis, "The library is open from 2 to 9 p.m. on Sundays," will not work because it requires no research beyond a telephone call or a look at the published schedule. But as every reader of detective fiction knows, a statement about time may take on significance for research. Even a seemingly unarguable hypothesis like

▼ The Declaration of Independence was signed July 4, 1776.

has been the subject of debate for a century and a half by those who argue that

▼ The Declaration of Independence was signed August 2, 1776.

(See Wilfred J. Ritz, "The Authentication of the Engrossed Declaration of Independence on July 4, 1776," *Law and History Review* 4 [Spring 1986]: 179–204.)

The third unworkable sentence, "I like broccoli," is unworkable not only because it needs no proof (for the author, at least) but because it is subjective. Personal likes or dislikes cannot be proven by evidence; they simply are. Broccoli, of course, is a legitimate topic of research when you have brought it to a hypothesis that can be tested. For example:

▼ Broccoli is nutritious.

▼ Eating broccoli helps prevent cancer of the gastrointestinal tract.

Notice that it is not the *I*, the grammatical first person, that makes "I like broccoli" unacceptable for a research paper, for the statement "Broccoli tastes bad" will not work either. That too reports an unverifiable subjective reaction, as do these other unworkable statements pertaining to emotions or sensory experiences:

I love the smell of star jasmine.

Twelve-tone music sounds harsh.

Squid has a repulsive feel.

This does not mean that tastes may not be studied. Psychologists, physicians, and public opinion pollers do research on tastes, as do advertisers and marketers of new products. It is possible, therefore, to imagine legitimate hypotheses like these:

▼ American college students dislike vegetables.

▼ When twelve-tone music was introduced, critics complained about its harsh sound.

For the purposes of a library research paper, this next condition is necessary:

2. Write a statement that can be tested by reference to materials in the library.

Here are some statements that will not work because of failure to meet the second condition:

Uncle Edward is the best storyteller in the family.

There are several places where I could have lost my pen.

My roommate has a mysterious past.

Professor Decker believes Shakespeare was old when he wrote *King Lear*.

These are all statements that could indeed be tested by research, but the library is unlikely to have any material to help you test them.

That is obvious for the first three, but what is the matter with "Professor Decker believes Shakespeare was old when he wrote *King Lear*"? There is nothing wrong with taking as a hypothesis the shorter statement:

▼ Shakespeare was old when he wrote *King Lear*.

though it would be a challenging statement to prove. But there is a problem with Professor Decker. As written, the hypothesis focuses on Professor

Decker's belief, not on the play. If Professor Decker is a literary scholar whose works on *King Lear* are in the library, fine. But unless the library happens to have books and articles by Professor Decker on *King Lear*, it won't be able to provide evidence for or against the hypothesis about Professor Decker's beliefs.

Turning to science, we encounter statements that are equally problematic. Little evidence exists in or out of a library to support any of the following speculations:

Intelligent life exists elsewhere in our galaxy.

Travel faster than the speed of light is possible.

It is possible to clone a human being.

For the present, these are statements of science fiction, not science fact. The facts that might support them remain to be discovered. Related statements that have given rise to such speculations may of course be useful hypotheses:

▼ Other planets in our solar system have climates which could support life.

▼ Travel that approaches the speed of light is technologically possible.

▼ Gene splicing permits the cloning of simple organisms.

Your library is unlikely to offer much in the way of sources for other more fantastic assertions:

Broccoli is an aphrodisiac.

The pyramids of Egypt were constructed with the help of ancient alien astronauts.

A Bigfoot family is hiding out in the Northwest Territories of Canada.

You will recognize these unsuitable hypotheses from the headlines of supermarket tabloids. They make claims about matters for which factual evidence is hard to come by, matters for which you will find ample opinions and anecdotes but little in the way of verifiable fact. Those who make the claims often write with great conviction, but it is not the vehemence of the writing or the offering of a few unverifiable anecdotes that provides the necessary evidence for a successful research paper.

You may, of course, propose a hypothesis dealing with people who hold, test, or oppose unverifiable beliefs. For example:

▼ The entrails of freshly slaughtered chickens guided Roman generals in their battle plans.

▼ The U.S. Air Force has found nothing extraterrestrial in its extensive study of UFOs.

A third basic condition for the research hypothesis is this:

3. Write an arguable statement: one that can be challenged, that is, one to which you can imagine possible objections.

The research hypothesis does not need to be controversial, but it does need to prompt a thoughtful reader to ask for explanation and evidence. With an arguable hypothesis, your work is clear: find the evidence that supports the hypothesis (or perhaps modifies it), and then write an explanation of the evidence you have found.

Consider these examples of unobjectionable, and therefore unacceptable, research hypotheses:

The earth's orbit is an ellipse.

The population of the United States was fourteen times larger in 1900 than in 1800.

Alice Walker writes about black women.

All three of these statements are true, and in each case it requires some research to demonstrate their truth: thousands of years of astronomical observations before Johannes Kepler determined the correct path of the earth's orbit, the door-to-door census throughout the United States to determine the population, and reading Alice Walker's fiction and essays to find out about her subject matter. But it takes no further research on your part to confirm any of these facts.

However, there are possible hypotheses that do express arguable opinions on these topics. For example:

▼ An unknown planet is the cause for distortions in the earth's elliptical orbit.

▼ A large increase in population changed the United States from a frontier society to a settled one in the nineteenth century.

▼ Alice Walker's strongest characters are black women.

For each of these satisfactorily revised hypotheses, it is possible to imagine objections. There could be some other cause for distortions in the earth's orbit, such as asteroids or a nearby star; some cause other than increased population for the closing of the American frontier; or strong male characters in Walker's writing. So those propositions call for research.

Here are further examples of unarguable and unacceptable hypotheses:

Professional sports derive large revenues from television.

Georges Seurat was a pointillist painter.

Pasteurization is a technique for sterilizing liquids.

Of course television provides lots of money for professional sports, but what of it? You might say

▼ Television has changed the style of play in professional sports.

—and for that statement you might imagine objections. The second and third of these unobjectionable statements are merely definitions. What point can you make about the pointillist?

▼ Georges Seurat's pointillism was a reaction to early impressionist painting.

And pasteurization? Objections could certainly be imagined to the hypothesis that

▼ Pasteurization substantially reduces the nutritional value of milk.

Look at scholarly articles and books for examples of this third condition. To a careless reader it may seem that an article in a scholarly journal merely offers information. The careful reader will discover that in most cases the article is making a point, very often arguing against a previously accepted view. Historians of the American Civil War once argued that slavery was the chief source of the conflict; later, others argued that the cause of the conflict between North and South was primarily economics; still later, others have argued again for the importance of slavery as an issue. Literary scholars argue over the interpretation of poems, even of single words; biologists debate the origin of life, while philosophers debate the meaning of it.

It is not absolutely necessary to take sides. After conducting your research, you may well find yourself writing a final thesis that sees merit in a variety of views, such as

▼ Authorities disagree about the causes of World War II.

▼ Evidence for the health hazards of electromagnetic radiation is inconclusive.

But your initial hypothesis gives better point and direction to your research if it is focused, as in these examples:

▼ The unfair Treaty of Versailles led to Hitler's election and World War II.

▼ Electromagnetic radiation poses no threat to health.

This third condition, that your hypothesis be arguable, is not as essential as the first two. It is possible to write a research paper on a proposition which nobody doubts, but which is complex enough to require explanation. The three earlier statements about professional sports, Seurat, and pasteurization are examples, and so are these:

▼ The angle of the sun accounts for the change of seasons.

▼ The gross national product of the United States has grown in the twentieth century.

Under some circumstances you may be permitted, or possibly even encouraged, to write on such a topic, but check with your instructor first. Why bother proving something that everyone agrees on already?

4. Avoid predicting the future.

Another unsatisfactory kind of hypothesis is one that looks to the future for verification:

The U.S. birth rate will continue to decline.

Alcohol will replace gasoline as a motor fuel.

Humans will colonize the planet Mars by the year 2025.

Vladimir Nabokov will be known as the greatest American novelist of the 20th century.

Iran will again become an ally of the United States.

If whale hunting is not prohibited, whales will become extinct in the next 20 years.

If funding for research were doubled, scientists would find a vaccine to prevent the common cold.

If journalists, the lowest-paid professionals, got higher wages, newspaper reporting would be more accurate.

Ending cost-of-living increases in wages and pensions would stop inflation.

An Equal Rights Amendment to the United States Constitution would improve relations between men and women.

What is wrong with these *wills* and *woulds*? Simply that they leave testing and evidence to the future or, in the case of *woulds*, to a world and time that may never come. In the year 2025 we will know whether humans have colonized Mars, but neither you nor your instructor can wait that long. And if journalists do not get higher pay, we will never know how much better our newspapers could be.

Again it is not hard to think of modified statements that could be tested. Look for a statement of current trends, not of what *will be* but of what *is:*

▼ The U.S. birth rate has been declining.

▼ The necessary technology is already available for colonizing Mars.

▼ Higher salaries are luring talented journalists from the media into public relations.

▼ Whale hunting continues to reduce the whale population.

▼ Cost-of-living increases have contributed to inflation.

▼ State equal-rights laws have resulted in equal pay for equal work.

These statements refer to events that have happened and can therefore be investigated.

And you need not avoid all mention of the future. The future can come in the concluding paragraphs of your research paper, where you let your reader know what is likely to follow from the trend that has been the point of your paper. But the heart of your research concerns itself with evidence of what now is, not speculation on what may happen.

5. Avoid negative statements.

This does not mean "think positive," but simply that it is wise to avoid saying that something is *not* the case; if so, you are not likely to find much evidence for it. To say "No cure has been found for the common cold" hardly requires research; a more fruitful hypothesis would suggest what has been done:

▼ Modern prescriptions work no better than traditional remedies to cure the common cold.

To say "Nuclear war has not occurred" is to state a simple fact not requiring further research. It would be better to write about precautions:

▼ The nuclear powers have many fail-safe mechanisms to prevent accidental firing of nuclear weapons.

6. Avoid unintended comparisons.

To say "Pittsburgh is the most livable city in the United States" is to require a comparison with all other cities in the country—something suitable for a book, but hardly possible in the limitations of a research paper. It would be easier to research and support the simple statement

▼ Pittsburgh is a livable city.

Similarly difficult are the comparisons implied in "Swimming is the best form of exercise" and "Emily Dickinson is the greatest American poet." The first hypothesis requires comparing all other forms of exercise with swimming, the second comparing all other American poets with Dickinson. Wait until you are ready to write a book.

7. Avoid statements that are actually topics in disguise.

Another kind of hypothesis to avoid is really not a hypothesis at all, just a topic masquerading as one. You can take any topic and make it into a sentence by adding "is important," "is controversial," "is a problem," or something grander like "is an important issue in American society today." Try it with any topic you like:

Deregulation of airlines is an important issue.

The federal budget deficit is a problem.

But to do this is to avoid a real hypothesis; a phrase like "is important" does not give the focus needed for efficient research. It's not much different from saying "Deregulation of airlines is a research topic." Yes, of course— but why?

That question is the way out of this difficulty. That is, you can convert those topics-in-disguise into true hypotheses by asking the question *Why:* Why is deregulation of airlines an important issue? Perhaps for one of these reasons:

▼ Deregulation of airlines leads to reduced air fares.

▼ Deregulation of airlines makes air travel more dangerous.

And why is the federal budget deficit a problem? Perhaps because

▼ The federal budget deficit raises interest rates.

8. Avoid a hypothesis that is too broad.

Hypotheses like "Exercise is healthful," "Crime is expensive," "Spain has a turbulent history" expect too much of your research. If you were writing a book, you could do justice to hypotheses like those, but for a medium-length research paper you will want to focus. For example:

▼ Running improves cardiovascular performance.

▼ Prisons are expensive to operate.

▼ The Islamic occupation of Spain left its mark on Spanish art.

Professional writers observe this limitation. Look at a newspaper or magazine, and you'll see articles with focused hypotheses: not "Pollution harms the environment" but

▼ Oil spills damage fisheries.

When the editors of *Time* or *National Geographic* want to argue that "The earth is endangered by humanity," they devote an entire issue to that thesis, with each individual article making a more limited point. Unless you have a few hundred pages in mind, limit your hypothesis too.

There is a ninth and final basic condition that your instructor may expect you to follow:

9. Write a proposition of fact rather than one of value or policy. (Avoid *should* or *must*; state what *is*.)

That is, your hypothesis will state that a certain factual situation exists. For example:

▼ First-born children are high achievers.

The hypothesis should not make a value judgment:

First-born children are nicer than others.

Nor should a hypothesis propose policy (though see the discussion on page 36 for an exception to this rule):

First-born children should be hired for leadership positions.

There is nothing wrong with propositions of value or policy. Many of the sources you find in the library will make such propositions, and you will be able to incorporate them as evidence toward your own factual hypothesis. But the fundamental activity of research is to establish what *is*. How you feel about the situation, or how you should feel, is a proposition of value; what should be done about the situation is a proposition of policy. But the explanation of the situation itself remains a matter of fact.

A research paper will report that the facts of a situation—historical and biographical reports, statistics, examples, scientific experiments—lead to a certain conclusion. An example of a proposition of fact is

▼ Smoking is hazardous to health.

This proposition claims that there is a cause-and-effect relationship between smoking and health, a claim that will need to be supported by factual evidence. The proposition of fact contrasts with "Smoking is evil," a proposition of value; and with "Smoking should be banned in public places," a proposition of policy.

The hypotheses used as examples in this book are propositions of fact. They make claims about existing circumstances ("Nuclear power plants are safe") or about knowable cause and effect ("Dreams are essential for mental health"). These are the kinds of propositions that scholars and scientists investigate.

A proposition of value, on the other hand, takes for granted that a certain situation exists, and says that it is good or bad, right or wrong, beautiful or ugly:

Classical music is better than popular music.

King Lear is Shakespeare's best play.

Euthanasia is wrong.

Terrorism against an unjust government is justified.

Since such propositions are based not on evidence but on beliefs and values, the proposition of value is not suitable for library research.

Religious beliefs are likewise unsuited for research because they are propositions of value. For example:

Cows are sacred.

Laziness (sloth) is a deadly sin.

Faith, not works, saves souls.

God created the world in six days.

There is one God, and Mohammad is his prophet.

Some of these statements look like propositions of fact. But they are supported by belief, not factual evidence. The faithful believe these statements not through research, but through accepting what is stated as the word of God. Sometimes this word is given by an intermediary like the Bible, the Koran, the church, or a minister. Sometimes it comes as a personal revelation. In either case, religious belief is not susceptible to proof, to either confirmation or denial by research.

But other matters relating to religion are grounds for research hypotheses because they are testable propositions of fact. Research is possible on theses like:

▼ Medieval theologians envisioned seven deadly sins.

▼ The doctrine of salvation by faith alone is central to Luther's beliefs.

▼ The Biblical story of the Creation has parallels in other ancient religions.

▼ Islam distinguishes itself from Christianity by its insistence on strict monotheism.

A third kind of proposition is the proposition of policy. It is easy to recognize because it uses the words *should* or *must*. The proposition of policy is a prescription, a statement that says what should be done:

The government should lower taxes to stimulate the economy.

The minimum age for driving should be raised to 18.

Women should get equal pay with men.

Like the proposition of value, the proposition of policy is not suitable for a basic research project, but for a different reason. Rather than not having anything to do with factual evidence, the proposition of policy goes further, requiring an extra step beyond the basic research paper. Underlying a proposition of policy is a proposition of fact, more suitable for research:

▼ Lowering taxes has stimulated the economy in the past.

▼ Drivers under age 18 are a hazard to themselves and others.

▼ Women and men do not get equal pay for equal work.

If you should want to write a proposition of policy, therefore, or if you should be assigned to do so, its place is not as a hypothesis for research but as a thesis for the conclusion of your research paper, after you have established the necessary underlying propositions of fact.

Here are other propositions of policy:

The United States and the Soviet Union should agree to end all testing of nuclear weapons.

Pornography should be banned.

Smoking should not be allowed indoors in public places.

American companies should not invest in South Africa.

The government must provide price supports for crops.

To move from these propositions of policy to their underlying propositions of fact, you can ask the question *why:*

Why should the United States and the Soviet Union agree to end all testing of nuclear weapons? Because

▼ Testing has led to the proliferation of nuclear weapons.

Why should pornography be banned? Because

▼ Pornography stimulates violence.

Why not allow smoking? Because

▼ Tobacco smoke harms ventilation machinery and individual health.

Why not invest in South Africa? Because

▼ American investment in South Africa strengthens apartheid.

In many cases, after establishing a proposition of fact, you will want to propose a policy, telling the reader what action should be taken in view of the information you have presented. This solves the problem of what to do for a properly emphatic conclusion to a paper based on a proposition of fact. A proposition of policy is appropriately placed at what should be the most emphatic part of your research paper, the very end.

With forewarning about the extra difficulty, however, it is possible that you may be permitted or even assigned to choose a proposition of policy. If so, do so—with the awareness that you must still demonstrate the underlying facts of the situation, and that you must also provide reasons why a policy will bring about improvement. Has it been tried? Has the alternative been tried? With what results? It is all too easy to make the hypothetical accord with one's wishes, and all too rare for a policy to work exactly as anyone expects. Do not lose your grounding in fact.

To summarize, before undertaking any research, you will save time and anguish by making sure that your hypothesis meets these nine key conditions:

CONDITIONS FOR THE HYPOTHESIS

1. Write a statement that requires testing.

2. Write a statement that can be tested by reference to materials in the library.

3. Write an arguable statement: one that can be challenged, that is, one to which you can imagine possible objections.

4. Avoid predicting the future.

5. Avoid negative statements.

6. Avoid unintended comparisons.

7. Avoid statements that are actually topics in disguise.

8. Avoid a hypothesis that is too broad.

9. Write a proposition of fact rather than one of value or policy. (Avoid *should* or *must*; state what *is*.)

Has your hypothesis passed the test? Does it meet these nine conditions? If so, you are ready to proceed to the next stage, the beginning of research. An assignment to help with the transition follows at the end of this chapter.

But what if, after all the effort of devising a good hypothesis, you find that your library doesn't have any articles or books that relate to it? Will you end up with hours of wasted searching?

Not likely. There is always that possibility, but the method of this book is designed specifically to avoid that waste. By thinking hard about your hypothesis and checking it against the conditions listed in this chapter, you have already greatly reduced the risk of ending up with a useless statement.

And there are further checks coming along. After refining your hypothesis, the next stage is a quick check of the reference sources available to you to see if there does in fact exist sufficient material to provide the evidence you need. As soon as you get to the library, you will be sent to an encyclopedia and then to other works in the reference collection to look for material relating to your hypothesis. If you find none, you will have lost only a few minutes of research time. You will then be able to change to another possible hypothesis with a minimum of wasted effort.

Now, however, after an exercise on types of statements, there is one further assignment to ensure the success of your hypothesis—a 500-word research proposal. This assignment has two purposes: to further reduce the risk of your choosing an unworkable statement, and to ensure that the hypothesis will remain central to your thinking as you look at what others have said. Furthermore, the arrangement of your thoughts about your hypothesis for this assignment will help guide the research you undertake and provide an outline for the research paper you eventually write.

EXERCISE 4.1

Determine which of the following statements are propositions of value or policy and thus unsuitable for a basic research paper (condition 9). Mark the propositions of value and policy with an asterisk (*) and for each write an underlying proposition of fact that would be suitable as a research hypothesis.

1. Genetic engineering is ethical.
2. Animals should not be used for scientific experiments.
3. The 1980s were the decade of freedom around the world.
4. The death penalty is immoral.
5. The Soviet Union should adopt a capitalist economy.
6. Gun control reduces crime.
7. Church and state should remain separate.
8. Science and religion are not compatible.
9. Nuclear war is not justifiable.
10. Drug testing should be mandatory in intercollegiate sports.

ASSIGNMENT II—500-WORD RESEARCH PROPOSAL

Write an informal essay of 500 words giving an explanation of your views in support of your hypothesis, based not on library research but on what you already know and what you think might be the case.

Put the hypothesis in a one-sentence paragraph of its own at the beginning—don't bother with a formal introduction. Then, in several paragraphs, make subpoints explaining the hypothesis in detail, telling what specific supporting evidence you hope to find. Finally, consider at least one possible objection to the hypothesis, and give your reply to that objection.

So that there can be no misunderstanding, label and separate the parts: first the single hypothesis in a paragraph by itself; next the explanation of the hypothesis in several paragraphs, each beginning with a subpoint; finally a statement of possible objections and your reply. Underline the hypothesis and the subpoints so that the outline of your paper is clear. Later, when you write an actual research paper, you will of course leave off the labels and the underlining and will use the more formal form described in Chapter 19.

What kind of evidence will you want to provide in your explanation of the subpoints? Above all, facts. There are two principal kinds of facts: evidence that sums up the entire subject and particular examples. If your hypothesis is

▼ Television watching weakens the academic performance of high school students.

you will want studies of the grades of groups of high school students as well as individual case histories. If your hypothesis is

▼ Freedom of expression promotes scientific progress.

you will want overall correlations of progress with freedom in various countries as well as specific examples of progress through freedom. If you propose that

▼ Air pollution is warming the planet.

you will want temperatures for the planet as a whole and some specific examples of places that are warming up, as well as information on the kinds and amounts of pollution. (Because this hypothesis deals with change, you will want evidence not just from the present but from earlier times as well, so you can show the trend.)

You are not expected to do research to come up with these pieces of evidence. If you happen to have done some background reading on the topic, fine; if not, your thoughtful ideas about what the evidence might be will serve perfectly well.

The evidence by itself does not make your point; you must present the evidence and explain how it relates to your hypothesis. This is the essential activity of writing a research paper, as we will see when we come to the chapters on writing about sources.

Organize subpoints according to the kinds of evidence you present. You may find it convenient to arrange your evidence by date, by type of case, by region or country, or by increasing breadth of coverage (starting with individual examples and moving on to general studies). If you are dealing with a change or trend, or with a historical event, you can organize the evidence chronologically. Organize carefully now, so you will later have ready-made places for the evidence you gather from your library research.

For this assignment, do not do additional research; simply write what you know and think. Do your best to imagine what the evidence will be, but do not worry whether every statement will prove to be true. The aim of this assignment is to clarify your own thinking before you begin your research. Because it requires so much thinking, it is not an easy assignment, but you will find it helpful later to have gone through the exercise of the research proposal now.

Two Examples

To see possible ways of fulfilling this assignment, look at the sample papers on the following pages. The labels make clear which part is which. Appropriately, the longest part of each paper is the explanation in the middle. Both happen to have four subpoints, but that number can vary depending on your own ideas.

Notice that, aside from being double-spaced, the proposals do not look like research papers—they have no title aside from the heading "Research Proposal," no citations of sources, no list of Works Cited.

The author of the first example has chosen a hypothesis that might have come either from reading or from personal experience. Perhaps the author read about Washington, D.C., or perhaps he or she visited the city. Thinking about the monuments leads to the conclusion that they must stand for something—and thus the hypothesis

▼ The monuments of Washington, D.C. stand for American ideals.

It is a hypothesis that will need some revision, if only because it is not specific about American ideals. Just what are they? Democracy or capitalism? One-person-one-vote or the Monroe Doctrine of opposition to European interference in the affairs of the Western Hemisphere? The subpoints give the author's answers to these questions; eventually, the hypothesis itself will have to specify the ideals.

The explanation gives specific subpoints, and supports each with facts and details. Actual research may turn up different facts and details, but at this stage a reasonable guess will do.

Notice that the paragraphs go in chronological order according to the subjects of the monuments. This arrangement could work for the research paper too.

S. Ward
English 202
April 4, 1991

RESEARCH PROPOSAL

HYPOTHESIS: The monuments of Washington, D.C. reflect
American ideals.

EXPLANATION: Four monuments come to mind, all reflecting
various ideals: the Washington Monument, the Jefferson
Memorial, the Lincoln Memorial, and the recent Vietnam
Memorial.

SUBPOINT 1:   The Washington Monument reflects the ideal
of unity. It shows the singleness of vision of the first
president, his unifying of thirteen separate former colonies
into a single nation. Although it honors Washington the man,
in it we find no statue or image of Washington, nor do we find
any of his deeds depicted or retold. Instead, the blank
monument standing tall above the city of Washington is itself
the image of his accomplishment in creating "one from many."

SUBPOINT 2:   The Jefferson Memorial reflects classical
ideals. In contrast to the grand Washington Monument is the
modest elegance of the memorial to Thomas Jefferson. It is a
round monument of perfect proportions in the ancient classical
style. The individual taught by the classics, inspired by the
free citizens of democratic Athens and republican Rome, self-
reliant, building with fellow citizens a perfect society in
the new wilderness—those are the Jeffersonian ideals suggested
by his monument.

SUBPOINT 3:   The Lincoln Memorial reflects concern for
the individual. It represents the human side of American
ideals, tempered by the somber experience of the Civil War.
Lincoln's understanding of American ideals of democratic
equality, of freedom, of concern for the individual, and of
unity are not merely suggested by his thoughtful pose but
written out on the walls of his memorial.

SUBPOINT 4:   The Vietnam Veterans Memorial reflects
ideals of equality, modesty, the worth of the individual, and
unity. This most recent and currently most visited of the
monuments of Washington is strikingly different from the other
three. Instead of accomplishment, it commemorates sacrifice
that led to no victory. Instead of one outstanding figure, it
commemorates thousands of individuals who never knew fame.
Nevertheless, it shares with the other memorials certain
American ideals: 1) equal opportunity and rights for all,
reflected in the listing of all of the Vietnam dead simply by

name and the order in which they died; 2) modesty rather than majesty, symbolized by the low wall and the absence of grandeur; 3) the worth of the individual, with each individual who died in the war being named; 4) the union of different individuals into one nation, one monument for all.

POSSIBLE OBJECTIONS: The monuments could reflect merely the notions of their designers. For example, since the Washington Monument is in the shape of an Egyptian obelisk, it could be argued that the designer wanted to represent Washington as a pharaoh. And the designer of the Vietnam Memorial may have meant it as an antiwar protest.

REPLY TO OBJECTIONS: But whatever private notions the architects may have had in mind, the monuments would not have been accepted unless the government and the public saw their designs as reflecting the ideals of the whole country.

Jamie Eshbaugh
Rhetoric 120J, Sec. 2
January 9, 1991

RESEARCH PROPOSAL

HYPOTHESIS: <u>American Sign Language is an effective</u> <u>language base for hearing-impaired children</u>.

EXPLANATION: Four aspects of language show the efficacy of American Sign Language, or ASL, as a language base for hearing-impaired children: concepts, role modeling, full expression, and linguistic rules.

SUBPOINT 1:   <u>American Sign Language promotes hearing-</u> <u>impaired children's conceptual accuracy</u>. The signs of ASL depict different meanings of words and phrases in different contexts.   The signs for a concept such as a nose running, running to the store, and running out of food are all signed in a different manner to maintain clarity and understanding for the child, despite the common word "run" in each.   Since children are constantly learning new vocabulary, the appropriate meanings would be crucial.

SUBPOINT 2:   <u>American Sign Language allows hearing-</u> <u>impaired children to role-model deaf adults</u>. Many deaf adults use ASL, so children can watch and learn the language. Proper use of vocabulary, grammar, and syntax can be taught to the hearing-impaired child through this method.   Deaf adult role models would also demonstrate formal and informal language patterns in the appropriate situations.

SUBPOINT 3:   <u>American Sign Language allows hearing-</u> <u>impaired children to express full thoughts and ideas</u>.   For many hard-of-hearing and deaf children, auditory and vocal methods are not feasible for full and free communication. ASL is a structured medium through which these children can explain their feelings, ask questions, and tell stories.

SUBPOINT 4:   <u>American Sign Language demonstrates</u> <u>adherence to linguistic rules for hearing-impaired children</u>. Obtaining proper understanding of the freedoms and limitations of one's own language, such as ASL, prepares a child for learning the rules of another language, such as English. Hearing-impaired children who have been using ASL for a few years could adapt better to the rules of English than those who have been trained orally or have no language skills at all.   Nouns, verbs, and other parts of speech are often analogous between the two, making the children's transition and learning less difficult than for other languages.

POSSIBLE OBJECTIONS: It could be argued that because ASL is a true language itself, it interferes with the learning of

English. Signed English or Signing Exact English could be
promoted to be better for teaching the hearing-impaired
English structure and the English language itself. Oral
proponents could argue that signs themselves hinder good
language and verbal skills.

REPLY TO OBJECTIONS: In general, the language of
hearing-impaired children is delayed, especially of children
who are educated through the strictly oral method. Signed
English and Signing Exact English are imitations of the
English language but not languages themselves. In addition,
they are not conceptually accurate or quick to use. Neither
the strictly oral method nor the English-like systems are used
by many deaf adults. The many linguistic aspects and wide
use, as well as its ability to be used with infants, make
American Sign Language a more effective language base than
these other systems.

$$\bigtriangledown$$

PART II

Finding Sources

▽

CHAPTER FIVE

POINTED WORDS

▽

Find key words for your research in the *Library of Congress Subject Headings.*

(The key words will be determined by your hypothesis; see Chapters 2, 3, and 4. Use the key words when looking in indexes; see Chapters 6, 7, and 8.)

▽

If you have thought through your hypothesis as carefully as Chapter 4 asked of you, chances are your library will offer abundant sources of evidence—books and articles giving facts, historical accounts, statistics, anecdotes, observations, and expert judgments—which will allow you to decide whether your hypothesis is true, or false, or true but in need of modification. Sit in the library, and chances are there are rich sources of relevant information just a short walk away. Walk around the library and they are likely to be so close you can touch them.

But these sources you need are hidden like the letter in Edgar Allan Poe's mystery story "The Purloined Letter," which escaped detection because it was concealed not in a secret place but among other letters. To solve the mystery and find sources that speak to your particular hypothesis, you will need to use reference works, including indexes and the library's own catalog.

And to look in general references, indexes, and the library catalog, you will need to find the key words—the subject headings—used by others. You will begin with the key words of your own hypothesis, but before you start looking through indexes you will need to make sure you are aware of other possible terms as well. If you do not have the right key words, or if you use only one word or phrase when there are several possible ones, you will fail to find material that could be available to you.

Some of your reference sources will be printed, some in computer databases (see Chapter 8). Whatever the form, you will need to develop a supply of key words before you begin searching.

Your hypothesis will already have its own key words. With the hypothesis

▼ Dreams are essential for mental health.

for example, "Dreams" and "Mental health" are key terms to use in indexes. With

▼ Lasers are beneficial in surgery.

we have "Lasers" and "Surgery" as prospective headings.

Others who write about these topics, however, may use other words. It is important at this beginning stage not to miss something that could be indexed another way.

But how can you know what other key words to use? Fortunately, there is a book that holds the answers. It is one that every library has for its own reference: the *Library of Congress Subject Headings.*

In the three volumes and 4463 pages of its 1989 edition, *Library of Congress Subject Headings* lists not only the 173,000 headings used by the nation's library, but also many other possible headings that a researcher might use. For most headings it also gives broader terms (coded BT) and narrower terms (coded NT), so that you can broaden your search if you want to find more material or narrow the search if you have too much.

Library of Congress Subject Headings (abbreviated *LCSH*) uses a simple alphabetical arrangement. You just look up a word or phrase in the alphabetical listing and see what other words are related to it. The words under each entry are coded to show the relationship to the headword:

USE—The Library of Congress *uses* the subject heading that follows.

UF—*Use* the boldface headword *for* this word. This word is not a subject heading used by the Library of Congress. It may, however, be used by other authors and indexers, so make a note of it.

BT—A *broader term* than the headword.

NT—A *narrower term* than the headword.

RT—A *related term*.

SA—*See also;* another headword that will have more information.

To get an idea of the richness of *Library of Congress Subject Headings,* look at the entries for "Lasers" (Figure 5-1). Lasers is used for (UF) three other terms; there are nine broader terms (BT), two related terms (RT), dozens of narrower terms (NT), and many subheadings and multi-word headings beginning with "Lasers." If you had the hypothesis

▼ Lasers are useful in medicine.

you would find not only the expected headings "Lasers in medicine," "Lasers—Diagnostic use," and "Lasers in surgery," but also "Holography in medicine,"

Laser spectroscopy
  UF Spectroscopy, Laser
  BT Lasers in chemistry
      Spectrum analysis
  NT Light beating spectroscopy
      Optoacoustic spectroscopy
      Photothermal spectroscopy
Laser transitions
  UF Transitions, Laser
  BT Lasers
Laser-using industries
  USE Laser industry
Laser welding
  BT Welding
Laser windows
  USE Lasers—Windows
Laser Writer (Printer)
  USE LaserWriter (Printer)
LaserJet printers
  USE HP LaserJet printers
Lasers *(May Subd Geog)*
  UF Light amplification by
      stimulated emission of
      radiation
      Masers, Optical
      Optical masers
  BT Infrared sources
      Light
      Light amplifiers
      Light sources
      Optical pumping
      Optoelectronic devices
      Photoelectronic devices
      Photonics
      Photons
  RT Astronautics—Optical
      communication systems
      Nonlinear optics
  SA *headings beginning with the*
      word Laser
  NT Atmosphere—Laser
      observations
      Carbon monoxide lasers
      Cartography—Laser use in
      Chemical lasers
      Dye lasers
      Far infrared lasers
      Fingerprints—Laser use in
      Free electron lasers
      Gamma ray lasers
      Gas lasers
      High power lasers
      Injection lasers
      Laser industry
      Laser interferometer
      Laser recording
      Laser transitions
      Laser in controlled fusion
      Laser in plasma diagnostics
      Laser in plasma research
      Metallurgy—Laser use in
      Mode-locked lasers
      Molecular gas lasers
      Negative temperature
      Neodymium glass lasers
      Nuclear-pumped lasers
      Plasma lasers
      Precipitation (Meteorol-
      ogy)—Laser observations

Printing, Practical—Laser
  use in
Rare earth lasers
Ruby lasers
Semiconductor industry—
  Laser use in
Semiconductor lasers
Solid-state lasers
Tunable lasers
— Diagnostic use
  BT Diagnosis
      Lasers in medicine
— Effect of radiation on
  UF Lasers, Effect of radiation on
  BT Radiation
— Military applications
  UG486
  BT Military engineering
      Weapons systems
— Mirrors
  UF Laser mirrors
  BT Mirrors
— Resonators
  UF Laser resonators
  BT Resonators
— Windows
  UF Laser windows
      Windows, Laser
Lasers, Argon
  USE Argon lasers
Lasers, Effect of radiation on
  USE Lasers—Effect of radiation on
Lasers, Excimer
  USE Excimer lasers
Lasers, Gasdynamic
  USE Gasdynamic lasers
Lasers, Helium-mercury
  USE Helium-mercury lasers
Lasers, Helium-neon
  USE Helium-neon lasers
Lasers, Iodine
  USE Iodine lasers
Lasers, X-ray
  USE X-ray lasers
Lasers (Sailboats)
  BT Sailboats
Lasers in aeronautics
  TL697.L34
  BT Aeronautics
Lasers in art
  N6494.L3
  BT Art
Lasers in biochemistry
  BT Biochemistry
Lasers in biology
  BT Biological apparatus and
      supplies
Lasers in biophysics
  BT Biophysics
Lasers in chemistry
  BT Chemical apparatus
      Photochemistry
  NT Laser spectroscopy
      Multiphoton processes
Lasers in controlled fusion
  BT Controlled fusion
      Lasers
Lasers in engineering
  BT Engineering

Lasers in isotope separation
  BT Isotope separation
Lasers in medicine
  R857.L37
  BT Medical instruments and
      apparatus
  NT Holography in medicine
      Lasers—Diagnostic use
      Lasers in surgery
Lasers in mining
  TN292
  BT Mining engineering
Lasers in ophthalmology *(May*
  Subd Geog)
  RE86
  UF Ophthalmic lasers
  BT Ophthalmology
Lasers in otolaryngology *(May*
  Subd Geog)
  RF51.5
  BT Otolaryngology, Operative
Lasers in physics
  BT Physics
Lasers in plasma diagnostics
  BT Lasers
      Plasma diagnostics
Lasers in plasma research
  BT Lasers
      Plasma (Ionized gases)—
      Research
Lasers in surgery
  RD73.L3
  BT Lasers in medicine
      Surgical instruments and
      apparatus
  RT Laser coagulation
  NT Laser lithotripsy
— Complications and sequelae
  (May Subd Geog)
Lasers in surveying
  BT Surveying—Instruments
Lasers in the graphic arts
  BT Graphic arts
LaserWriter (Printer)
  UF Apple LaserWriter (Printer)

Figure 5-1

"Lasers in ophthalmology" and "Ophthalmic lasers," "Lasers in otolaryngology" and "Otolaryngology, Operative" and several others.

Or consider the hypothesis

▼ Dreams are essential for mental health.

What does *Library of Congress Subject Headings* tell us about dreams?

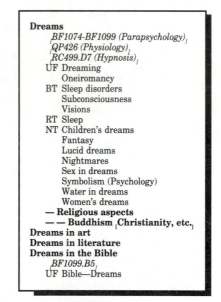

```
Dreams
     BF1074-BF1099 (Parapsychology)
     QP426 (Physiology)
     RC499.D7 (Hypnosis)
  UF  Dreaming
      Oneiromancy
  BT  Sleep disorders
      Subconsciousness
      Visions
  RT  Sleep
  NT  Children's dreams
      Fantasy
      Lucid dreams
      Nightmares
      Sex in dreams
      Symbolism (Psychology)
      Water in dreams
      Women's dreams
   — Religious aspects
   — — Buddhism ¡Christianity, etc.¡
Dreams in art
Dreams in literature
Dreams in the Bible
     BF1099.B5
  UF  Bible—Dreams
```

Figure 5-2

Under the heading Dreams (Figure 5-2), *LCSH* gives two UF terms—Dreaming and Oneiromancy—which might be used by other authors and indexes.

It gives three broader terms (BT): Sleep disorders, Subconsciousness, and Visions.

It gives one related term (RT): Sleep.

It gives eight narrower terms: Children's dreams, Fantasy, Lucid dreams, Nightmares, Sex in dreams, Symbolism (Psychology), Water in dreams, and Women's dreams.

In addition, it indicates subheadings having to do with the Religious aspects of dreams in Buddhism, Christianity, and so forth. And it even indicates three subject categories that include dreams: Parapsychology, Physiology, and Hypnosis.

These are all possible headings to use when searching through indexes and catalogs. However, with a hypothesis that says "Dreams are essential for mental health," most of these seem irrelevant. The broader topic *Sleep disorders* seems most useful for further searching.

Physical education and training
(May Subd Geog)
GV201-GV555
UF Athletic training
Education, Physical
Physical culture
Physical training
Sports—Training
Sports training
Training, Physical
BT Education
RT Athletics
Calisthenics
Exercise
Gymnastics
Sports

SA *individual types of exercises,
e.g.* Fencing; Rowing;
Running; *also subdivision*
Physical training *under
classes of persons and under
individual military ser-
vices, e.g.* Fire fighters—
Physical training; United
States. Army—Physical
training; *and subdivision*
Training *under individual
sports, e.g.* Football—
Training
NT Coaching (Athletics)
College sports
Delsarte system
Drill (not military)
Executives—Physical training
Exercise for men
Games
Jiu-jitsu
Motor learning
Movement education
Music in physical education
Nudism
Physical education for men-
tally handicapped persons
Physical education for women
Physical fitness
Physical fitness for men
School sports
Sports sciences
Swedish gymnastics
T'ai chi ch'üan
Television in physical education
Wages—Physical education
and training
Weight training
—Ability testing
USE Physical fitness—Testing
—Early works to 1800
UF Athletics—Early works to
1800
Sports—Early works to 1800
—Law and legislation *(May Subd Geog)*
—Medical aspects
USE Sports medicine
—Moral and ethical aspects
UF Physical education and
training— Moral and
religious aspects
—Moral and religious aspects
USE Physical education and
training— Moral and
ethical aspects
Physical education and
training— Religious aspects
—Religious aspects
UF Physical education and
training— Moral and
religious aspects
——Buddhism, ┌**Christianity, etc.**┐
—Safety measures
GV344
NT Sports—Accidents and injuries
—Teacher training
USE Physical education
teachers— Training of
—Testing
USE Physical fitness—Testing

Physical fitness *(May Subd Geog)*
Here are entered works on
muscular efficiency and physical
endurance. Works on optimal
physical, mental, and social well-
being, as well as how to achieve
and preserve it, are entered
under Health.
UF Endurance, Physical
Fitness, Physical
Physical endurance
Physical stamina
Stamina, Physical
BT Exercise
Health
Physical education and
training
Sports sciences
NT Astrology and physical
fitness
Bodybuilding
Circuit training
Muscle strength
—Nutritional aspects
—Religious aspects
——Buddhism, ┌**Christianity, etc.**┐
—Testing
GV436
UF Physical capacity
Physical education and
training— Ability testing
Physical education and
training— Testing
BT Ability—Testing
Anthropometry
Physical fitness and astrology
USE Astrology and physical
fitness
Physical fitness centers
(May Subd Geog)
UF Health clubs
Health spas
Spas
BT Physical education facilities
Recreation centers
NT Home gyms
—Law and legislation
(May Subd Geog)
Physical fitness for children
(May Subd Geog)
RJ61
BT Children
NT Bodybuilding for children
Physical fitness for men
(May Subd Geog)
UF Men—Physical fitness

Figure 5-3

As an example of cross reference, consider the hypothesis

▼ Athletic training improves body responses.

If we look under "Athletic training" in *LCSH*, we are told to USE "Physical education and training." Under that heading (Figure 5-3), we find dozens of related and narrower terms. The narrower term that seems closest to the hypothesis is "Physical fitness." Turning to the entry for that heading, we find another helpful feature of *LCSH*, an explanatory note: "Here are entered works on muscular efficiency and physical endurance. Works on optimal physical, mental, and social well-being, as well as how to achieve and preserve it, are entered under Health." So "Health" will be another key word to consider when looking for sources relating to that hypothesis.

No matter what your hypothesis, the *Library of Congress Subject Headings* can help. If the hypothesis is "Mary Shelley's novel *Frankenstein* reflects modern attitudes towards science," you will need no special instructions to look under "Shelley, Mary" and *"Frankenstein."* But what about modern attitudes toward science? The *LCSH* entry for Attitudes refers us (USE) to "Attitude (Psychology)" and to the related term "Public opinion." Under "Science," in turn, we find the subheadings "Philosophy" and "Social aspects." A note there refers us also to the heading "Science and civilization."

Take as another example a relatively recent term, "Sports medicine." In older works you would have to use different headings. What might they be? *Library of Congress Subject Headings* offers a number of possibilities. *LCSH* uses "Sports medicine" for (UF) "Athletic medicine"; "Athletics—Medical aspects"; "Medicine, Sports"; "Medicine and sports"; "Physical education and training—Medical aspects," and "Sports—Medical aspects." There are also narrower terms (NT) "Athletes—Medical examinations," "Athletes—Nutrition," "Doping in sports," "Equine sports medicine," "Pediatric sports medicine," "Sports—Accidents and injuries," and "Sports ophthalmology."

Chapter 4 offered a 500-word essay illustrating the hypothesis "The monuments of Washington, D.C. illustrate American ideals." For this hypothesis *LCSH* provides, under the heading "Monuments," among others the related terms (RT) "Memorials and Public sculpture," and the narrower terms (NT) "National monuments" and "War memorials." Under "Ideals (Aesthetics)" we are directed to the broader term (BT) "Aesthetics," which refers to values in art, and under "Ideals (Philosophy)" to the broader term (BT) "Philosophy." Turning to the heading "Washington (D.C.)," we find a subheading "Monuments," a combination that brings together two of the terms of the hypothesis. The term "Memorials," in turn, has a subheading "Washington (D.C.)" with three narrower terms (NT) that are the first three examples mentioned in the 500-word essay: "Lincoln Memorial (Washington, D.C.)," "Thomas Jefferson Memorial (Washington, D.C.)," and "Washington Monument (Washington, D.C.)." Under "Lincoln Memorial (Washington, D.C.)" we find another broader term (BT): "National parks and reserves—Washington (D.C.)." The term "War memorials" likewise leads to the subheading "Washington (D.C.)" and the narrower term (NT)

"Vietnam Veterans Memorial (Washington, D.C.)." So even if the author of the original hypothesis did not know which memorials were to be found in Washington, *Library of Congress Subject Headings* would lead from the hypothesis to the particular memorials.

As new words make their way into the news, *LCSH* incorporates them in its new editions. If a newly prominent key word does not appear in *LCSH*, you may be able to find it in the supplemental *L.C. Subject Headings Weekly List*, also put out by the Library of Congress. While the term *perestroika* was too new for the *LCSH* in 1989, it did find a place on the *Weekly List*, with a brief definition ("Here are entered works on the restructuring of Soviet society initiated by General Secretary Mikhail Gorbachev") and reference to broader terms "Soviet Union—Economic policy—1986-" and "Soviet Union—Politics and government—1985-." Those terms, in turn, lead to two pages of headings for the "Soviet Union" in *LCSH*.

These examples of *Library of Congress Subject Headings* could go on and on. It is a fascinating tool, showing the interrelationships among the subjects we deal with in research. But the best way to proceed is not with this book but with *LCSH* itself. Find a place where you can spread out the three heavy volumes and browse through them. We conclude this chapter with an exercise and then the assignment that has you use *LCSH* in connection with your research paper.

It should be noted that *Library of Congress Subject Headings* is not the only place to find key words. Most fields of study have their own dictionaries and indexes of terms. In psychology, for example, the *Thesaurus of Psychological Index Terms* lists 4500 headings used in *Psychological Index*. Be alert to other terms used by those who write on the subject of your hypothesis. Be alert to names, too: places and especially people associated with your hypothesis, whether as participants or as authors of studies.

EXERCISE 5.1

Part I

By referring to *Library of Congress Subject Headings*:

1. Find two other terms for "Dental hygiene."
2. Find four other terms for "African Americans."
3. Find another key word for "Adolescents."
4. Find nine other terms for "Developing countries."
5. Find another key word used for (UF) "Disabled." Find how many narrower terms (NTs) are used under those headings.
6. Find seven other terms for "Tennis elbow."
7. Find a key word to use for the "Afterlife."

Part II

For each of the terms in the exercise at the end of Chapter 2, look through *Library of Congress Subject Headings* to find at least half a dozen related, broader, or narrower headings. You may follow references from one entry to another in order to get the needed number of key words.

It may be necessary to begin the search with a word other than the one on the list. For example, *Library of Congress Subject Headings* does not mention Tickling as a topic. You might look under "Play," or the related term (RT) "Amusements," or the narrower terms "Playmates" or "Recreation"—or "Child psychology" and the narrower terms found there of "Aggressiveness (Psychology) in children," "Interpersonal relations in children," "Senses and sensation in children," "Social interaction in children." There is also the heading "Child abuse," with the alternates (UF) "Child maltreatment" and "Cruelty to children."

ASSIGNMENT III

After acquainting yourself with the format and method of *Library of Congress Subject Headings*, use it to make a list of key words for your own research hypothesis. Start with the words of the hypothesis and see what related, broader, and narrower terms *LCSH* provides. From these, select terms that relate to the whole of your hypothesis, discarding irrelevant ones, as in the examples of "Dreams are essential for mental health" and "Athletic training improves body responses" given in this chapter. These key words are the key to finding source materials, so take time to be thorough and precise.

Works Cited in Chapter 5

L.C. Subject Headings Weekly List Issue 12 (22 March 1989).

Library of Congress Subject Headings. Prepared by Subject Cataloging Division, Processing Services. 12th edition. 3 volumes. Washington, D.C.: Cataloging Distribution Service, Library of Congress, 1989.

Thesaurus of Psychological Index Terms. 4th edition. Washington, D.C.: American Psychological Association, 1985.

▽

CHAPTER SIX

INTRODUCTION TO RESEARCH: THE REFERENCE ROOM

▽

Get acquainted with your subject using a general encyclopedia and other reference works. To locate relevant material, look in the index.

(Make use of all suitable key words, Chapter 5. If you are already well acquainted with the subject, proceed to look for sources for your paper, Chapter 7.)

▽

With a well-thought-out hypothesis and a list of key words, you are now at the end of the beginning of the research process. Next come the three stages involving research sources: finding them, writing about them, citing and listing them.

Later chapters will treat each of these activities separately. But they must be performed together each time you use a source, so it is necessary to mention them all before going into detail on each one. This chapter therefore offers an introduction to all three stages.

To introduce the activities of finding, writing, citing and listing, this chapter will make use of introductory sources, those that a researcher naturally looks for at the start of a research project. Unless you are already expert on a subject, you will begin your research most efficiently in a place specifically designed to help you find quick answers and gain an initial orientation to a field—the library's reference collection.

Before you look at your subject in depth, you need to obtain a general understanding of the field. If you do not, the articles and books in depth are likely to be too deep for understanding, or out of context. To use a simple analogy, it helps to have a map when you are looking in new territory. The "maps" of books, periodicals, and other sources—of the knowledge available in a library—are found in the reference room. Later research will lead you to various corners of the library and beyond, but it begins here.

THE GENERAL ENCYCLOPEDIA

The search begins where almost any search can begin, with the most accessible of reference sources, the general encyclopedia. Beginning with an encyclopedia is efficient in two ways. First, it eliminates uncertainty about where to start; you can always start with an encyclopedia. Second, it immediately informs you whether you are likely to have difficulty finding sources for your hypothesis. If you find material relating to your hypothesis in an encyclopedia, there is likely to be an abundance of relevant sources elsewhere in the library. If, on the other hand, you do not find relevant material, even after searching the encyclopedia index with all the key words you have found for all the parts of your hypothesis, you will know at once that you will need a revised or different hypothesis. You will have wasted no time on dead-end research.

In fact, going to an encyclopedia is what the experts do when they take aim at an unfamiliar subject. The professional researchers, librarians, and scholars who have no time to waste start with an encyclopedia or handbook to get an overview and only then move on to specialized sources.

The general encyclopedias of repute include the *World Book*, *Americana*, *Collier's*, *Academic American*, and the scholarly *Britannica*. Of these, the easiest to start with is *The World Book*. It is a favorite of librarians at all levels for its simple presentation, accurate information, and attentiveness to current issues. The opening paragraph of a *World Book* article is generally couched in language a high school student can understand; as the article develops, more difficult concepts and terminology are presented. It is a logical way to be introduced.

Should you always go to *The World Book* first? Not necessarily. You may find the other general encyclopedias just as convenient. Each has something distinctive to offer. With several encyclopedias at hand, you may simply prefer to use the one that is most up to date. To find out the date of publication, open any volume of the encyclopedia, turn to the back of the title page, and look for the most recent year of copyright. That will be the year in which that edition of the encyclopedia was published.

Using the Index First

Whichever encyclopedia you use, turn first to the index. It is a separate volume or two at the end of the set, and its function is to guide you to every place where information on a given topic may be found, not just the heading for that topic in the main alphabetical listing. The evidence may be scattered through many articles; only the index will lead you to all articles that treat your subject.

Using the index is especially important for the general encyclopedia that gets the greatest respect in academic circles, *The New Encyclopaedia Britannica*, 15th edition. The *Britannica* entries come in two separate alphabetical listings: the short quick-reference entries of the *Micropaedia* and long comprehensive entries of the *Macropaedia*. Fortunately, a comprehensive two-volume index at the end of the *Britannica* refers you to both listings. (Until the 1985 edition, the *Micropaedia* served not only for quick reference but also as the index. If your library has a pre-1985 *Britannica* 15th edition, it will have no separate index and you will have to start with the *Micropaedia* instead.)

That is only one of the ways the *Britannica* stands out from the rest. Of the five general encyclopedias, the *Britannica* is distinguished both for high reputation and for difficulty of use. Its reputation is such that, alone among general encyclopedias, the *Britannica* is likely to be an acceptable reference in your final research paper.

The scholarly articles of the *Britannica* are in the *Macropaedia* section of longer entries. The *Micropaedia* section of short entries, on the other hand, competes with the other general encyclopedias as a source of quick reference and brief introduction to a topic.

Encyclopedia Article vs. Research Paper

As you begin looking through encyclopedias, keep in mind one important difference between an encyclopedia article and a research paper. The research paper makes a point; the article does not. Instead, the encyclopedia article provides raw material for research to the point. A research hypothesis, for example, may state that

▼ Penicillin is an effective antibiotic.

Under the heading Penicillin, an encyclopedia will provide information relating to that hypothesis, but also much else: information about its discovery, discoverer, effectiveness, side effects, and history of use.

The encyclopedia tries to cover every question a reader might ask. But a research paper focuses on one point only—your point. So the encyclopedia is not your model for a research paper; it is the raw material.

Within the encyclopedia that you choose, you will be looking for works that offer something in regard to your hypothesis—some evidence in support of it, or opposed to it, or in support of a modified version of the hypothesis. Something is all that's necessary. You will rarely find a reference work that is entirely relevant to a hypothesis, first because reference sources generally cover more territory than you would cover in a hypothesis, and second because most reference sources cover topics rather than theses. Very often you will find in a source only a paragraph, or even just a sentence or two, or a few facts that help support or clarify your hypothesis. Providing you can connect that information to your hypothesis, that is all you need.

Once you find relevant material, you will want to write about it—to explain what support (or opposition) it provides for your hypothesis—and to cite and list the source, so your reader will know exactly where you got your material. Chapters 9 through 11 will explain citing and listing, and Chapters 12 through 16 will explain the writing, but here we will present an overview of the process and an assignment which gives you practice.

An Example: Finding and Writing

As a simple example, let us take the previously illustrated hypothesis

▼ The monuments of Washington, D.C. represent American ideals.

Key words developed in Chapter 5 lead us to a number of entries in *The World Book*, including those for the city and for individual monuments. In the volume with letters W-X-Y-Z, Volume 21 of a recent edition of *The World Book*, the index directs us to a long article with the title "Washington, D.C." Skimming that article, we notice photographs and paragraphs for each of the four monuments discussed in the 500-word research proposal at the end of Chapter 4. Do these paragraphs have any evidence we could relate to the hypothesis? Figure 6-1 shows the paragraph on the Washington Monument. Is there anything here that provides evidence in regard to the thesis?

> **Washington Monument** is a towering, slender, white marble *obelisk* (pillar) dedicated to the memory of George Washington. The tallest structure in Washington, D.C., it rises 555 feet 5$\frac{1}{8}$ inches (169.29 meters). An elevator inside carries visitors to the top. From there, a person can see much of the Washington area.

Figure 6-1

At first glance the answer to this question would seem to be no. Nothing in this short paragraph directly mentions American ideals. But our instructions are to look for sources of information to support, oppose, or modify the hypothesis. We do not need *statements* related to the hypothesis, just *information*. So let us look for information about the monument that could be relevant.

Consider, then, the fact that the Washington Monument is an obelisk, which (the dictionary will tell us) is a sloping pillar with a pyramid top—a simple unified design. In using our own words to explain the relevance of this design to the hypothesis, we could point to an ideal of unity:

EXAMPLE 6.1

As Eunice S. Grier and Atlee E. Shidler state in The World Book Encyclopedia, the Washington Monument is in the shape of an obelisk (74). This simple design symbolizes the unifying of the thirteen sovereign states into one nation under Washington's leadership.

Works Cited

Grier, Eunice S. and Atlee E. Shidler. "Washington, D.C." The World Book Encyclopedia. Chicago: World Book, Inc., 1990. 21: 70-88.

It will be useful to take a careful look at Example 6.1 and the other examples in this chapter, because they are examples of what to do from now on every time you find a relevant source.

Notice, first of all, that Example 6.1 begins by naming the authors and the encyclopedia. This is to make perfectly clear, from the beginning, the source of information.

The first sentence of the example then presents a fact from the source—a specific fact about the shape of the Washington Monument. But facts alone do not constitute an explanation. So what if the Washington Monument is an obelisk? What does that have to do with American ideals?

The answer to these questions is the responsibility of the researcher. Hence the need for the second sentence about the obelisk, one that explains the relation of the source information to the hypothesis.

That is the point of research: telling what the source says (the first sentence, in this case) in order to support (or oppose, or modify) the thesis (the second sentence). You, the researcher, make the connection.

Notice also that not all of what the encyclopedia tells about the monument is relevant to the thesis. The shape of the monument has to do with its symbolism, and consequently it is mentioned in the example. But the elevator has nothing to do with what the monument symbolizes, so we do not mention it.

Documentation: Citing and Listing

The other aspect of using a source is what we call documentation. It has two parts: citing sources and listing them.

Citing takes place in the sentences you write about the source. Citing means telling the reader who provided the information and exactly what page or pages it came from. So it always involves two items: the name of the author or authors and the page number or numbers. In Example 6.1, the sentences of explanation begin with the authors' names. The page number then is given in parentheses at the end of the first sentence making use of the source.

Citing requires author and page number. Other information is optional, to be included if it will help the reader understand what sort of source you are using. Example 6.1 informs the reader that the source is an encyclopedia.

Citing author and page number is all you do in your sentences, but you need to provide further information to guide the reader to a copy of your source. This information goes in an alphabetical list of Works Cited at the end of your paper. Example 6.1 shows the publication information needed for listing an article in an encyclopedia, arranged in this order: author's name, encyclopedia name, edition of encyclopedia (if stated on title page— if not, omit), city of publication, name of publisher, year (latest year of copyright), volume, and pages.

Page numbers receive different treatment in citing and listing. You cite only the page or pages that provide the specific material you are using (74, in Example 6.1), but you list the full range of pages of the article (70–88). Further examples of citing and listing will be given below, and a complete explanation will come in Chapters 9 through 11.

The authors' names, essential for citing and listing, are easy to overlook. Before you decide that an article names no author, look carefully around. Most articles, even short ones, do have a signature.

Where do you find the authors' names? In encyclopedias, these generally come at the end of articles. Or the names will be hidden near the end of an article, just before a list of further readings. Often, furthermore, the names of authors are in small print. Look at the small type used for James J. Cullinane's name in the source for our next example.

Another Example: Finding, Writing, Citing and Listing

In addition to its article on Washington, D.C., *The World Book* has a separate entry for the Washington Monument itself (Figure 6-2).

Some of the information in this entry can be related to the thesis on American ideals, some cannot. The measurements, the elevator and stairs, the cost, the engineering, and the dates of construction and dedication do not seem relevant. But then there is the matter of the stones. Couldn't this be evidence of unity from diversity, another American ideal? Let us then say it:

EXAMPLE 6.2

As James J. Cullinane states in <u>The World Book Encyclopedia</u>, the Washington Monument includes inside its walls 189 stones contributed by diverse individual constituents of the American republic and foreign countries, including private citizens as well as cities and states (110). Cemented within the simple obelisk of the monument, these stones symbolize the American ideal of unity from diversity, one from many.

Washington Monument is a great obelisk built in honor of George Washington. It stands in Washington, D.C., near the Potomac River, about halfway between the Capitol and the Lincoln Memorial.

The monument has the shape of the obelisks of ancient Egypt, but it is several times larger than they were. It is 555 feet 5 1/8 inches (169.29 meters) high, and measures 55 feet 1 1/8 inches (16.79 meters) along each of its four sides at the bottom. The sides slant gradually inward as they rise to the base of the *pyramidion* (small pyramid) which tops the pillar. At this point, each side of the pillar is 34 feet 5 1/2 inches (10.50 meters) long. The pyramidion rises 55 feet (16.8 meters). The walls of the monument are 15 feet (4.6 meters) thick at the bottom and 18 inches (46 centimeters) thick at the top. They are covered with white marble from Maryland. The stones covering the pyramidion are 7 inches (18 centimeters) thick. A cap of cast aluminum protects the tip.

Inside, the monument is hollow. The inner walls are set with 189 carved memorial stones, many of historic interest. The stones were presented by individuals, societies, cities, states, and other countries. Visitors must take an elevator to the top of the monument. To descend, they can either take the elevator or walk down the 898 steps leading from the top. The view of Washington, D.C., is impressive. More than a million people visit the Washington Monument each year.

Some people planned a memorial to Washington while he was still alive, but he objected to the expense. In 1833, the Washington National Monument Society began raising funds for a monument. A design by Robert Mills had already been accepted in part. The government approved the project, and the cornerstone was laid on July 4, 1848, with the same trowel that Washington had used to lay the cornerstone of the Capitol in 1793. But engineers found the ground too soft, so they moved the site to the north.

Many people donated stones for the monument. Pope Pius IX sent a marble block from the Temple of Concord in Rome. One night in 1854, a group believed to be Know-Nothings, or members of the American Party, stole this block (see **Know-Nothings**). This act shocked the public, and contributions almost stopped. In 1855, Congress agreed to give some financial aid to the project. But Know-Nothings broke into the society's offices and claimed possession of the monument. In 1876, Congress voted to finish the project at government expense. Work began on Aug. 17, 1880. It was completed on Dec. 6, 1884. The monument was dedicated on Feb. 21, 1885, and opened to the public on Oct. 9, 1888. Its total cost was $1,187,710.31. The monument is maintained as a national memorial by the National Park Service.

James J. Cullinane

Figure 6-2

```
                    Works Cited
Cullinane, James J.   "Washington Monument."   The World
     Book Encyclopedia.   Chicago: World Book, Inc., 1990.
     21: 110-111.
```

That is one way of writing about this source. It is important to realize that it requires the researcher's own thinking and interpretation. And because it is the researcher's thinking, not the source's, there can be more than one appropriate interpretation. Example 6.3 is a different but equally correct explanation of evidence from the same source:

```
                    EXAMPLE 6.3
     To the outside world the Washington Monument
symbolizes American unity.  But on the inside, as James
J. Cullinane states in The World Book Encyclopedia, the
monument displays examples of American diversity, with
189 inscribed stones contributed by groups and individu-
als, states, and foreign countries (110).  The importance
of these stones as a symbol of American diversity was
illustrated in 1854 when a group presumably opposed to
Catholicism stole a stone contributed by the Pope (111).
According to The World Book, the public was shocked at
this violation of the American ideal of inclusiveness
(111).

                    Works Cited
Cullinane, James J.   "Washington Monument."   The World
     Book Encyclopedia.   Chicago: World Book, Inc., 1990.
     21: 110-111.
```

In Example 6.3, there are four sentences, and three of the four explain the connection of source material to the thesis. There are many possible ways to arrange the sentences you write about a source. Notice, though, that the listing of Works Cited is the same as in Example 6.2. It gives the full pages of the article, whether or not the citation in the sentences makes use of all the pages.

This example shows also that in citing a source you include the page number in parentheses at the end of the *last* sentence making use of that page as well as the first, if you use it for more than one sentence. And when you change pages, you put the new page number at the end of the first sentence making use of that new page, as well as the last.

An Example from the *Britannica*

For a final example of writing about a source, let us try the most scholarly of the general encyclopedias, *The New Encyclopaedia Britannica*, 15th edition. Its index leads us to, among other things, a quick-reference *Micropaedia* entry on the Jefferson Memorial, complete with photograph. The text of the article appears in Figure 6-3.

Jefferson Memorial, formerly THOMAS JEFFERSON MEMORIAL, monument on the south bank of the Tidal Basin, Washington, D.C., authorized in 1934 and dedicated April 13, 1943, the 200th anniversary of Pres. Thomas Jefferson's birth. The memorial, set in 18 ac (7 ha), is a unit of the National Capital Parks and a site in the five-point plan for central Washington, which includes also the Capitol, White House, Washington Monument, and Lincoln Memorial. The circular-colonnaded structure, designed by John R. Pope, Otto R. Eggers, and Daniel P. Higgins, was built in the classical style that Jefferson preferred. The pediment over the portico depicts Jefferson reading his draft of the Declaration of Independence. In the centre of the domed marble-lined interior is a heroic bronze figure of Jefferson sculpted by Rudulph Evans; inscriptions of his writings appear on the four interior panels and frieze.

The memorial appears in its most picturesque setting in early spring when the Oriental cherry trees, encircling the Tidal Basin, are in bloom.

Source: Reprinted with permission from *Encyclopaedia Britannica,* 15th edition, © 1987 by Encyclopaedia Britannica, Inc.

Figure 6-3

Here again we find quite a collection of facts, many of which we cannot use as evidence relating to the thesis about American ideals. The date of authorization of the memorial and the names of its designers do not suggest a connection with American ideals. But details of the memorial and its setting can be seen as relevant. We are told that the memorial is set in an 18-acre park surrounded by cherry trees; that it has a classic design; that the decorations include the Declaration of Independence and excerpts from Jefferson's writings. What American ideals do these hint at? Something different from Washington's, certainly. Possibly this:

EXAMPLE 6.4

Though it lies in the midst of the nation's capital, the Jefferson Memorial suggests a preference not for cities but for the peaceful countryside, not for crowds of people but for the independent individual. The New Encyclopaedia Britannica notes that the Jefferson Memorial is located not in an urban environment but in an 18-acre park, further set off by the cherry trees of the Tidal Basin which bloom in the spring ("Jefferson Memorial" 523). Also emphasizing support for individual independence is the depiction on the monument of Jefferson working on the Declaration of Independence (523).

```
                        Works Cited
"Jefferson Memorial."  The New Encyclopaedia Britannica.
    15th edition.  Chicago: Encyclopaedia Britannica,
    Inc., 1987.  6: 523.
```

This time three sentences explain how evidence in the source can be connected to the hypothesis. Note once more that the connection to the thesis is not made by the source; all that the encyclopedia provides is evidence about the memorial's location and design. It is up to the researcher to make the connection between evidence and thesis. That is what a research paper is all about.

Notice also a difference in documentation. These sample sentences cite the title of the encyclopedia article, in quotation marks, as well as the page number. That is because no author is given for the article. The citation in the sentences must include whatever comes first in the Works Cited listing. In this case, lacking identification of an author, the listing begins with the next element, the title of the article. That must be cited in the sentences so the reader can connect with the right listing.

It should be clear from the examples that you always cite author and page *even though you are using your own words* instead of quoting the words of the source.

It should also be noted that the listing states "15th edition" because that fact is mentioned on the title page of the encyclopedia. No edition was mentioned for *The World Book* in Examples 6.1 through 6.3 because the title page made no mention of edition.

Mysteries of the *Britannica*

Citing the *Britannica* involves extra difficulty. (The difficulty perhaps enhances the *Britannica*'s scholarly reputation.) Please notice:

—All of the entries in the *Micropaedia* are unsigned; no author is named. You will therefore have to put the title of the entry in parentheses when citing the source, as in Example 6.4.

—The *Macropaedia* does indicate authors' names at the end of articles, but only by their initials. To find authors' full names, you need to look in the index of authors, which is in a separate volume called the *Propaedia*.

Updating the Encyclopedia

No matter how recent the edition, an encyclopedia cannot give us today's news, this month's research report, the current year's statistics. Of course, that information should not be overlooked. But usually that can come later. At the time of starting out, your purpose is to get an overview of the evidence relating to the hypothesis, including an understanding of developments in the past. The very latest reports you can save for later, when you can put them in perspective against this background.

If you have chosen a reasonably recent edition of an encyclopedia, therefore, you need not be concerned at this point with updating its information. But the question of timeliness becomes more urgent if you have written a hypothesis about something so recent that it is not mentioned in the encyclopedia at all.

Fortunately, the encyclopedia offers its own remedy to the problem of keeping up with the news: a supplement known as a yearbook or book of the year. Every major encyclopedia publishes updating yearbooks. Not only do they give the developments of each year shortly after the year is over, but they also provide summaries and statistics for the year which are never included in the main encyclopedia. So if you are following a hypothesis which tells of change or development, you may want to look through yearbooks for a number of different years to see how each treats the same material.

A yearbook will enable you to begin with an encyclopedia even for a recent topic. Suppose, for example, you decided in 1987 to write on the hypothesis

▼ The Chernobyl accident shows that nuclear power is hazardous.

In *The New Encyclopaedia Britannica*, 1987 edition, the index gives no entry for Chernobyl at all—neither as city nor as location of a power plant, let alone as the site of radioactive explosions in April 1986. But you can find material about Chernobyl in the *1987 Britannica Book of the Year*. The index to that yearbook lists 28 different places where Chernobyl is mentioned. Using that yearbook, you would have no trouble finding information for a sentence like this:

EXAMPLE 6.5

The explosions in only one reactor at Chernobyl, according to the <u>1987 Britannica Book of the Year</u>, were hazardous enough to bring harm to most of the northern hemisphere. The accident caused 31 deaths and the evacuation of 135,000 people. The Chernobyl accident also contaminated much of Europe, Asia, and North America with radioactivity. Some sheep in northern England and Scotland, for example, became too radioactive to be sold for meat (Allaby 221).

Works Cited

Allaby, Michael. "Environment." <u>1987 Britannica Book of the Year</u>. Chicago: Encyclopaedia Britannica, Inc., 1987. 218-223.

That is just one example of evidence for the hazards of the Chernobyl accident; the yearbook provides many more.

Whether you use the encyclopedia itself or a yearbook, the assignment at the end of this chapter will give you practice in writing about the encyclopedia sources you find for your own thesis.

THE REFERENCE COLLECTION

General encyclopedias are only the tip of the iceberg. A reference collection will contain many other convenient sources of information.

Before you study particular works by experts, you need to get the general picture, and a generally accepted overview of a topic is just what a reference work aims to provide.

Furthermore, a specialized book often is written to emphasize one particular view, sometimes even to challenge accepted opinion. You need to know what the generally accepted view is before you can properly handle challenges to it.

A search through the reference collection, like the encyclopedia investigation, will serve two essential purposes. It will help you determine, first, whether your hypothesis is likely to hold up or needs modification; and second, whether there is likely to be sufficient library material relating to the hypothesis, modified or not. Thus it will save you both time and frustration.

If there are materials in the library, the reference collection ought to know about them. It's the brain that knows about the larger body of materials in the body of the library (and indeed in the other libraries of the world).

The reference room is likely to store another kind of brain on hand: the computer database, on disc or on line. You will want to explore those too; see Chapter 8 for an orientation. But one drawback to the computer databases is that you cannot see them. The best way to gain an awareness of the references available to you is still to look at the printed reference works.

There is no prescription for the way to get acquainted with the reference collection. Your library itself will have its own ways of orienting you, generally including floor plans and guides to reference works. Perhaps your instructor, or a friendly librarian, will arrange a tour. But there is no substitute for looking over the reference collection on your own, at your own pace and with your own interests and research hypothesis in mind. You will be wise to budget an hour in the beginning just for preliminary browsing.

In that hour, walk around the room and see for yourself what is there. Don't just look at the volumes on the shelves; pick out a few and browse through them. Notice the grouping of particular types or subject matter at particular sections, shelves, and tables. Here are a few you are likely to encounter.

Dictionaries and Specialized Encyclopedias

In one place you will find dictionaries—everything from short dictionaries of slang to the scholarly *Dictionary of American Regional English*, the *Barnhart Dictionary Companion* (a periodical reporting on new words) and the great *Oxford English Dictionary*, just published in twenty big volumes of its second edition. (Some libraries will instead have the first edition of twelve volumes, with four volumes of a supplement). All three of these dictionary sources have special value for the researcher because they are historical; that is, they show the histories of words by giving examples from earliest use to the present. Much more than mere definitions, they show the development of words and their associated ideas through the years. (For bibliographic information on the reference works mentioned here, see the list of Works Cited at the end of this chapter.)

Along with these historical dictionaries, or in the different subject-matter areas of the reference collection, will be many dictionaries of particular subjects. They are useful not only for orienting you to a subject, but for suggesting additional key words for your search. There are specialized dictionaries of law, medicine, business and finance, politics, the underworld, biology, chemistry, computer science, music, ballet, film, and Islam—just to name a few.

Another section of the reference collection, with which you should already be familiar, will hold the general encyclopedias, from the convenient one-volume *New Columbia Encyclopedia* and its new smaller cousin *The Concise Columbia Encyclopedia* to the massive scholarly New *Encyclopaedia Britannica*.

But there are also numerous specialized encyclopedias, excellent for providing an expert perspective while orienting you to a field. To take some examples, there are specialized encyclopedias dealing with art, science, the social sciences, history, literature, education, philosophy, the Bible, Catholicism, Judaism, the Soviet Union, and many more. If you are writing on Mozart's early career, for example, you will want to look not only at the general encyclopedias and biographies but also at the music section of the reference collection, in works like the twenty-volume *New Grove Dictionary of Music and Musicians*.

People, Places, Statistics, Current Events

Biographies for the whole world, and for particular nations, times, and occupations, will have their corner in the reference collection. They deserve particular attention, because people are almost as useful as key words in leading you to sources of further information.

Lives of the truly famous will be in *Current Biography*, the prominent in the various *Who's Who*s, anyone who makes the headlines (including many sports figures) in *The New York Times Biographical Service*. Specialized biographical works give information on present-day scholars and scientists (perhaps including faculty members at your institution), artists, composers, women, African Americans, and people in many other categories; historical collections tell of prominent people of various nations, some (like the *Dictionary of American Biography*) with lengthy articles. There are many works about contemporary authors, most notably more than one hundred volumes of *Contemporary Authors*. In addition to alphabetical listings and indexes in the works themselves, you can use the periodical *Biography Index* to locate entries in some of these works, as well as biographies published elsewhere.

In the reference collection you will also find geographical reference works, including maps, atlases and gazetteers (geographical dictionaries). Some of these do far more than show where places are located; they show history, natural resources, population, and trade and commerce, for example.

You will find statistical works in the reference collection, one of the most useful being the *Statistical Abstract of the United States*, which is published in a new edition every year by the U.S. Bureau of the Census. The census taken every ten years is itself published in many volumes of analysis, also often found in the reference room. Other statistics, as well as historical facts, appear in annuals like the *World Almanac*.

The *World Almanac* is closely related to another kind of work found in many places in a reference collection, the handbook. A handbook is a miniature encyclopedia, and handbooks are available for almost every conceivable subject: higher education, aging, chemistry and physics, nursing, classical drama, and the literature of various nations, for example. Among the literary handbooks you will find also plot summaries of novels, plays, and poems.

For information on current events, you might think you would have to go to a different part of the library and check the current periodicals. In fact, however, that will be necessary only for the most recent events. Reference rooms keep up to date with such serial publications as *Current Biography*, *Facts on File* (a reference digest of world news), and *Historic Documents*. General encyclopedias, you will remember, are kept up to date with volumes known as yearbooks, which organize and summarize developments year by year.

All these are sources that provide alphabetically or topically organized information for quick reference. Their indexes, as well as their alphabetical listings, will be open to your key words (and key names, in the case of biographical works). Thus they are ideally designed for a first check on the soundness and testability of your hypothesis. Thankfully, the library has brought all these works together in one room or area for your convenience—and they cannot be checked out, so they will always be available to you.

The arrangement of reference works in your library's reference collection is not haphazard. They will be shelved systematically by type and topic according to a standard classification, usually the Library of Congress system (whose codes for different subjects start with the letters A–Z) or the Dewey decimal system (numbered 000–999). A reference librarian will almost certainly be able to provide you with an outline of your library's classification system. Carry it around as you go from section to section, and make notes on what you find where.

One relevant source can lead you to others. It can suggest other related topics, other works on the topic, and people associated with the topic—as well as additional key words to use as you search through indexes.

Guide to Reference Books

As you consider which reference sources to use and wonder how reliable they are, you can ask your instructor or reference librarian for help. But you can get expert help on your own, too. Somewhere in the reference room you will find the source that librarians themselves use: Eugene P. Sheehy's *Guide to Reference Books*. This thick book tells about most of the materials you will find in even the largest reference collection. It not only lists thousands of reference works by category and topic but also has a paragraph explaining and evaluating each one. Select the topic that relates to your hypothesis and start reading in Sheehy. Then, after you find listings of works that seem useful, look them up in your reference room catalog.

The *Guide to Reference Books* can also be of help in determining whether a reference source is available in a computer database. A large black dot following an entry in that guide indicates that at least part of the reference work is available on line or on compact disc. (For information on computer searches, see Chapter 8.)

In-depth References

While most reference material is designed to provide general overview and quick answers, some in-depth material may be available in the reference collection too: for example, collections of historical documents, speeches, even of literary criticism (*Contemporary Literary Criticism*).

Indexes, Bibliographies, Abstracts, and the Library Catalog

There is one other kind of work in the reference collection: the work that, instead of providing explanations itself, directs you to the in-depth studies you will need for your research paper. These guides are the indexes and bibliographies, the sources that point the way to materials that are not in the reference room but elsewhere, in the main collections of your library and of other libraries. Without these indexes you could wander among library collections for days and never find an article or book relating to your hypothesis; with the indexes, you know exactly where to go. Among the many indexes, the most widely known is the *Readers' Guide to Periodical Literature*. But that is only the tip of the iceberg. Here is a short list of some of the better-known ones:

American Statistics Index

Art Index

Bibliographic Index

Biography Index

Business Periodicals Index

Cumulative Index to Nursing and Allied Health Literature

Current Index to Journals in Education

Education Index (includes physical education)

Essay and General Literature Index (an index to books that are collections of essays, rather than to periodical articles)

General Science Index

Humanities Index (includes literature, language, the arts, history, philosophy, and religion)

Index Medicus

Index of Economic Articles

Index to Free Periodicals

Index to U.S. Government Periodicals

International Index (to 1965; predecessor of *Social Science and Humanities Index*)

International Nursing Index

Library Literature

MLA International Bibliography (literature, language, folklore)

Music Article Guide

New York Times Index (of articles in the *Times)*

Nineteenth Century Readers' Guide

Physical Education Index

Physical Fitness / Sports Medicine

Poole's Index to 19th Century Literature

Public Affairs Information Service (PAIS)

Readers' Guide to Periodical Literature

Social Science and Humanities Index (1965-1974; successor to *International Index*, predecessor to the current separate *Humanities Index* and *Social Science Index)*

Social Science Index (includes psychology, sociology, social work, anthropology, political science, geography, economics, law and criminology)

Wellesley Index to Victorian Periodicals (of the 19th century; see *Nineteenth Century Readers' Guide* and *Poole's Index)*

Some of the indexes to other works contain so much information that they can be used as quick reference sources in themselves. *The New York Times Index,* for example, provides a detailed chronological summary of each year's news in all subject areas, as well as an index to all articles published in that newspaper. And before you check out books in the library's general collection, you can learn quite a bit about some of them from the index known as *Book Review Digest.* As its name indicates, it includes excerpts from published reviews of books, together with information on the content of the books. Other indexes that will lead you to books include

Book Review Index

Current Book Review Citations (to 1982)

Index to Book Reviews in the Humanities

NLS Cumulative Book Review Index

Before you take the trouble to get copies of books and articles, there are quite a few reference sources that will not only direct you to these books and articles but also summarize what is in them. *The New York Times Index* and *Book Review Digest* are two we have already mentioned. Looking at these summaries will save you the labor of getting a copy of a source only to find that it is not relevant to your hypothesis.

The summaries are generally called abstracts. A collection of abstracts is called an abstracting index. One such reference work that covers all fields is *Dissertation Abstracts International,* which has summaries of all American doctoral dissertations and some foreign ones. Dissertations are book-length scholarly and scientific studies on the frontiers of new knowledge. You might be surprised at how many thousands there are each year.

Here are some of the other abstracting indexes:

Biological Abstracts

Chemical Abstracts

Child Development Abstracts and Bibliography

Current Awareness in Health Education

DSH Abstracts (deafness, speech, hearing)

ERIC Abstracts

ERIC Resources in Education

Psychological Abstracts

Readers' Guide Abstracts (abstracts of articles indexed in the *Readers' Guide*)

Sociological Abstracts

All have indexes by subject, suitable for using the list of key words you have developed from *Library of Congress Subject Headings* and your other reading.

One other basic reference source that you will shortly be using is the library's catalog. The next chapter discusses it further.

As you look through reference sources to acquaint yourself with the subject of your research hypothesis, it can be good preparation to practice writing about the sources and then citing and listing them. Whether the source is a general encyclopedia or an in-depth study in a scholarly journal, the procedure is the same. The exercises preceding the assignment provide opportunity for practice with all three stages of using sources.

EXERCISE 6.1—ENCYCLOPEDIA REPORT

Using the key words you developed in the last chapter, look in the index of a general encyclopedia for articles with evidence relating to your hypothesis. When you have found relevant evidence, write about it in the following way:

On a sheet of paper, write your hypothesis, so that you (and your instructor) will have it clearly in mind. Then, following Examples 6.1 through 6.5, write one or more sentences that state the evidence and explain its relevance. Avoid direct quotation; use your own words to explain the evidence, not the words of the source. Cite author and page in your sentences, and list the source in a Works Cited entry with full publication information.

Finally, make a photocopy of the specific page or pages from which you have obtained the relevant evidence. Mark the place on the photocopy that gives the evidence and hand in both your notes and the photocopy.

At the end of this chapter a worksheet for the encyclopedia report is given, along with an example of one that is filled in. You may use this form or plain notebook paper. Or your instructor may ask you to put your sentences on large index cards (4x6 or 5x7 inches) and your Works Cited listing on small index cards (3x5).

EXERCISE 6.2—REFERENCE REPORT

Do the same as the previous exercise, but use a specialized reference work rather than a general encyclopedia.

If your source is an article in a book, the Works Cited listing will look much like that for an article in an encyclopedia. For example (an article without a named author; if there were an author, the author's name would go first):

```
"Hungary."  The World Almanac and Book of Facts 1990.
     New York: World Almanac, 1989.  717-718.
```

If, on the other hand, your source is an article in a periodical—something published in different issues on different dates, like a magazine, newspaper, or scholarly journal—the listing will look like this:

```
"Vietnam War Memorial Dedicated."  Facts on File 42 (19
     November 1982): 863.
```

For a periodical, you do not need to state city or publisher, but you do include volume number (42, in the example above), exact date of issue (19 November 1982), and full page or pages of the article (this is complete on one page).

Again, this example does not have an author indicated for the article. If it did, the entry would begin with the author's name.

Forms for both kinds of reference sources are given in Appendix II. Fuller explanation of listing and citing is given in Chapters 9, 10, and 11.

ASSIGNMENT IV—BACKGROUND FOR RESEARCH

Using the key words you developed in Chapter 5 with the help of the *Library of Congress Subject Headings*, and using the encyclopedia's index volume to locate appropriate articles, look in a general encyclopedia for evidence relating to your hypothesis: evidence to support, oppose, or modify it.

If you do not find information, ask help from your instructor or a reference librarian to make sure you have not overlooked any key words or approaches. If there still is no information, modify your hypothesis and try again.

When you find relevant information, read it. Take notes on additional key words and names that appear in the article, for use with future indexes. If the article has a bibliography listing other articles and books on the topic, make a note of those that seem relevant to your hypothesis. Be sure to note full publication information, not just author and title. (See Chapter 9 for specifics on what information is needed.)

With that, you are ready to look further afield. The next chapter will lead you to the in-depth sources that will be the heart of your research.

Works Cited in Chapter 6

(Note: Periodicals are listed by title only, and the titles of indexes listed in the middle of this chapter are not repeated here. See Chapter 9 for full explanation of Works Cited listings.)

Academic American Encyclopedia. Danbury, Connecticut: Grolier Incorporated, 1988. (An updated version is published each year. The latest copyright year on the back of the title page is the year of publication for that particular version.)

Barnhart Dictionary Companion.

Book Review Digest.

Collier's Encyclopedia. New York: Macmillan Educational Company, 1989. (An updated version is published each year. The latest copyright year on the back of the title page is the year of publication for that particular version.)

The Concise Columbia Encyclopedia. Edited by Barbara A. Chernow and George A. Vallasi. 2nd edition. New York: Columbia University Press, 1989.

Contemporary Authors. Detroit: Gale, 1962-present.

Contemporary Literary Criticism. Detroit: Gale, 1973-present.

Current Biography Yearbook: 1986. Edited by Charles Moritz. New York: H. W. Wilson Company, 1987. (A new volume is published each year, in addition to the monthly periodical issues. Each volume will have different years in the title and publication date, and possibly a different editor.)

Dictionary of American Biography. Edited by Allen Johnson and Dumas Malone. 20 volumes. New York: Charles Scribner's Sons, 1928-37. Supplements edited by various editors. 7 volumes. New York: Charles Scribner's Sons, 1944-1981. (Each volume will have a different publication date, and possibly a different editor. The series of supplements is continuing.)

Dictionary of American Regional English. Edited by Frederic G. Cassidy. Volume 1, A-C. Cambridge, Massachusetts: Belknap Press of Harvard University Press, 1985.

The Encyclopedia Americana. International Edition. Danbury, Connecticut: Grolier Incorporated, 1988. (An updated version is published each year. The latest copyright year on the back of the title page is the year of publication for that particular version.)

Facts on File.

Historic Documents of 1987. Washington, D.C.: Congressional Quarterly Inc., 1988. (A new volume is published each year. Each volume will have different years in the title and publication date.)

Library of Congress Subject Headings. Prepared by Subject Cataloging Division, Processing Services. 12th edition. 3 volumes. Washington, D.C.: Cataloging Distribution Service, Library of Congress, 1989.

The New Columbia Encyclopedia. Edited by William H. Harris and Judith S. Levey. New York: Columbia University Press, 1975.

The New Encyclopaedia Britannica. 15th edition. Chicago: Encyclopaedia Britannica, Inc., 1987. (An updated version is published each year. The latest copyright year on the back of the title page is the year of publication for that particular version.)

The New Grove Dictionary of Music and Musicians. Edited by Stanley Sadie. 20 volumes. London: Macmillan Publishers Limited, 1980.

The New York Times Biographical Service.

The Oxford English Dictionary. Edited by James A. H. Murray, Henry Bradley, W. A. Craigie, C. T. Onions. 1st edition. 12 volumes. Oxford: The Clarendon Press, 1933. Supplement edited by R. W. Burchfield. 4 volumes. Oxford: The Clarendon Press, 1972–86.

The Oxford English Dictionary. Prepared by J. A. Simpson and E. S. C. Weiner. 2nd edition. Oxford: The Clarendon Press, 1989.

Sheehy, Eugene P. *Guide to Reference Books.* 10th edition. Chicago: American Library Association, 1986.

U.S. Bureau of the Census. *Statistical Abstract of the United States: 1987.* 107th edition. Washington, D.C.: U.S. Government Printing Office, 1986. (Each volume will have different years in the title and publication date.)

Who's Who 1985–1986. Volume 137. New York: St. Martin's Press, 1985. (Lists people from all over the world, but chiefly Great Britain. Each volume will have different years in the title and publication date.)

Who's Who in America. 44th edition, 1986–87. 2 volumes. Wilmette, Illinois: Marquis Who's Who, 1986. (Each edition will have different years in the title and publication date.)

The World Almanac and Book of Facts 1990. New York: World Almanac, 1989.

The World Book Encyclopedia. Chicago: World Book, Inc., 1990. (An updated version is published each year. The latest copyright year on the back of the title page is the year of publication for that particular version.)

▽

ENCYCLOPEDIA REPORT WORKSHEET

Hypothesis _____

_____

_____

   How does the material in this source support (or modify or oppose) the
hypothesis?

   _____

_____

_____

_____

_____

_____

_____

_____

_____

_____

_____

_____

_____

_____

Entry for list of Works Cited (follow this model):

```
Last Name of Author, First Name or Names. "Title of
     Article."  Name of Encyclopedia. Edition. City,
     State: Publishing Company, Year. Volume: Complete
     pages.
```

_____

_____

_____

_____

ENCYCLOPEDIA REPORT WORKSHEET

Hypothesis American Sign Language is an effective language base for hearing-impaired children.

How does the material in this source support (or modify or oppose) the hypothesis?

American Sign Language provides clarity for hearing-impaired children. As Willard J. Madsen describes it in The World Book Encyclopedia, "ASL is based on ideas rather than words" (453). Because of this reliance on ideas, hearing-impaired children will understand concepts and meanings first. With this background, English words will be more easily comprehended.

Due to the importance of concepts, every English word does not correlate to a sign (Madsen 453). To remedy this, Madsen states that signs are used along with fingerspelling to lend specificity to certain terms (453). The ability to be specific or general would broaden the range of topics easily discussed. Also, the ability to spell would be important for the reading and writing of hearing-impaired children. These aspects would support ASL as an effective language base.

Entry for list of Works Cited (follow this model):

> Last Name of Author, First Name or Names. "Title of Article." Name of Encyclopedia. Edition. City, State: Publishing Company, Year. Volume: Complete pages.

Madsen, Willard J. "Sign Language." The World Book Encyclopedia. Chicago: World Book, Inc., 1990. 17: 453–454.

CHAPTER SEVEN

SOURCES IN DEPTH

▽

Sources that support, oppose, or modify the hypothesis must be of sufficient quantity, variety, timeliness, and quality. To find sources, consult indexes and catalogs, and look for bibliographies that lead you to other sources.

(Chapter 8 discusses the use of computer databases to find research sources. When you have found a source, cite and list it [Chapters 9–11] and write an explanation of its relevance to your hypothesis [Chapters 12–16].

▽

Your actual research paper needs sources of a different sort than the general reference works of the previous chapter. To be convincing, you need information in depth, and if possible first hand: from eyewitnesses of a historic event, scientists conducting experiments, legislators debating an issue, or scholars who have thoroughly reviewed the first-hand information. A research paper persuades not in the fashion of advertisements by making bold assertions, but in the manner of scholars and scientists by offering and considering the best available evidence and weighing all sides of a question. The sources you use should reflect that thoughtful attitude.

FOUR CRITERIA
FOR SOURCES

Above all, so that you and your reader will be able to say that your paper is well-researched and well-supported, these sources of evidence and opinion in regard to your hypothesis must be of sufficient *quantity, variety, timeliness,* and *quality*. Let us consider those requirements in order.

1. Quantity

First of all, quantity. A research paper needs a considerable number of sources. If it makes use of only one or two sources, no matter how good they are, it becomes little more than a summary of those sources; the one or two sources take control of the paper's approach and point of view and do not allow the author sufficient independence of judgment. (To avoid uncritical following of a persuasive source is one reason for forming a hypothesis before you begin research.) The number of sources needed for sufficient quantity depends on your hypothesis and the material you find, but for a typical 2500-word research paper, a dozen sources beyond the reference room would ordinarily be a reasonable minimum.

Depending on how much information each provides, a dozen sources might also be a sufficient maximum for a paper of that length. Increased numbers of sources will not necessarily make a better paper, just as eating twice as many calories as you need will not necessarily make you twice as healthy.

2. Variety

More than quantity, what matters with your dozen or so sources is their variety, timeliness, and quality. Variety simply means that your dozen or so sources should come from at least half a dozen or so different places. They should not all be periodicals, for example, nor should they all be books. Periodicals present information one way and books another, and both ways are valuable. Periodicals generally emphasize the new and timely; books take a more comprehensive view. Periodical articles tend to focus on particular points; books can range more widely and deeply. So you need both kinds.

Furthermore, your periodical sources should not all come from the same newspaper, magazine, or journal. The authors of the articles may be different, but the articles will always have to meet that journal's set of editorial standards. Your paper needs material that has been judged by a variety of standards.

The same principle of variety holds for book publishers, even when the publishers are distinguished university presses. A certain publisher will become known for publishing books that take a certain approach, so it is important to get books from a variety of publishers.

So, for example, in the field of linguistics (the study of language), one publisher may favor books that show the distinctive characteristics of particular languages, while another publisher favors studies of universal qualities characteristic of all languages. Both kinds of studies are valid. It is not a question of one being wrong and the other being right. Rather, it is a question of having sufficient variety in the sources so that your final thesis will have support from more than one point of view.

Variety, then, is necessary. As a rule of thumb, if you have a dozen sources, you should have no more than two sources from any single book publisher or periodical (magazine, scholarly journal, or newspaper). An exception might be made for the leading scholarly journal or scholarly publisher in a field, but the exception would be to allow no more than three or four items with that imprint, and to make sure in compensation that the remaining items are well scattered in their origins.

Primary and Secondary Sources

Another way in which sources differ is by type, primary and secondary. Not all hypotheses lend themselves to both kinds of sources, but when possible, having both will make for considerable variety in points of view. Examples of primary sources are a letter by Abraham Lincoln, President Nixon's secret tape recordings, an edition of Emily Dickinson's poems, the journals of Lewis and Clark, a case study by Sigmund Freud, census records, a list of the sign language gestures used by a chimpanzee, the Magna Carta, court transcripts, the text of legislation, the *Congressional Record*, the book or film of *Gone With the Wind*, the patent application for the electric incandescent light, the diary of Anne Frank, or a record of observations of Halley's Comet.

Secondary sources are scholarly and scientific studies: a biography of Lincoln, a study of Watergate, an analysis of Emily Dickinson's imagery or correspondence, a study of population trends, a discussion of the linguistic ability of a chimpanzee, a study of recent Supreme Court decisions, a report on the influence of special-interest lobbying on legislation, the diagnosis of an illness and discussion of treatment for it, an analysis of the nature and probable origins of Halley's Comet.

3. Timeliness

A third dimension for sources, after quantity and variety, is time. Since you are writing for a present-day audience, at least some of your sources must be timely; they need to reflect present-day understanding and attitudes, even of phenomena that are timeless (like the structure of crystals) or events that happened long ago. For some fields, like the politics of Eastern Europe, present-day may mean the latest day's news, available in newspapers, on radio or Cable News Network, or through on-line databases (for those, see Chapter 8). For many other subject areas, like the investigation of life on other planets, the physiology of exercise, or the development of commercial air travel, present-day is within the last two or three years; and for some subjects on which attitudes have changed little, perhaps horseshoeing or calligraphy, you may be able to go back many years for current attitudes.

Even so, without at least a few recent sources, a research paper is subject to the suspicion of being outdated. This is true also for the study of cultural and historical events and figures of long ago: There are new views of Shakespeare's plays and of the American Civil War that are not the same as those of 100 or 50 years ago. The reputation of artists and political leaders continues to rise and fall long after they are dead.

Not all of your sources have to be new. Since a research paper examines a hypothesis in depth, the depth of time may give it a useful perspective. Moreover, if you use primary sources, they must be close in time to the original events or situation rather than to the present day. But to assure that you have not overlooked recent developments, at least a few up-to-date sources are necessary.

In fact, the right up-to-date source can be a key to all of your research. Its references can lead you to other present-day studies as well as to the most important earlier ones.

4. Quality

The most important—and most difficult—criterion for your research paper sources is quality. For the research paper you will look for specialized studies in depth and first-hand reports of researchers and eyewitnesses.

The sources of highest quality for a research paper most often are the works of other researchers, that is, research studies aimed at scholars and scientists. They appear in scholarly journals and in books by university and academic presses, both of which have the same sort of requirements for stating and documenting sources as your research paper. In fact, the research paper is patterned after articles in scholarly and scientific journals.

That does not mean nonacademic sources must be avoided. You can legitimately make use of *National Geographic*'s detailed report on an Alaskan oil spill or the restoration of the Sistine Chapel frescoes; a cover article in *Time* on cholesterol or a special issue on 150 years of photojournalism; a *Wall Street Journal* report on new styles of job interviews or marketing milestones of the 1980s; *New York Times* accounts of the opening of the Berlin Wall or a Supreme Court decision. If you are not an expert already on a subject, both you and your reader will find such material easier to understand and explain than a highly technical journal article intended for other experts.

But sources aimed at a general or popular audience are to be used with caution. A pamphlet on recommended diet from the American Cancer Society is at some distance from a scholarly review of studies of diet, nutrition, and cancer. The complexities and uncertainties of the situation as viewed by scientists will necessarily be simplified and smoothed over in a pamphlet intended to provide guidance to the consumer.

When you write a research paper, you are seeking evidence and expert analysis, not looking for entertainment. So when you are studying the causes of heart disease, look for a medical journal rather than a pamphlet from the county health department. When you are writing about the fuel efficiency of modern automobiles, look for government studies and *Consumer Reports* tests, not the brochures offered by car dealers.

Specialists in a field will turn exclusively to scholarly journals and books for their own research. Ideally, you would do the same. But that is a difficulty if you are new to a field. Such works are often difficult to read and understand unless you are a specialist yourself. You may very well, therefore, desire to compromise and get at least some sources that are addressed to a more general audience.

Here is where you must use careful judgment. Much is published that is too general, too simplified, and thus not suitable as a source for a research paper. Especially suspect are publications intended mainly for entertainment, recreation, or instruction, publications whose aim is to amuse or teach the reader or promote a hobby or special interest rather than to inquire about the truth.

You will not need to be told that supermarket tabloids like *The Globe, Weekly World News*, and *National Enquirer* are not sufficiently scholarly to serve as sources for a research paper. They will not even be in your library. Though the *National Enquirer* claims to conduct an independent verification of every story, its standards of verification are not quite the same as those of a scholar or scientist. So you cannot simply take the *Enquirer*'s word that a creature from another planet has been working as an astronaut for the Soviet Union.

Moving up in quality, you must also not rely on consumer-oriented "popular" magazines for a research paper, even though they are more soberly written. *Better Homes and Gardens, Sunset, Field and Stream, Glamour, Good Housekeeping, People Weekly, Popular Mechanics, Popular Photography, Popular Science*, to take a few examples—these offer good advice, but that is different from the spirit of searching inquiry that is appropriate for academic research. An exception is *Consumer Reports*, a popular magazine with first-hand research reports on consumer items and no advertising to cast doubt on the independence of its judgments.

A Guide to the *Readers' Guide*

The periodical indexes listed in Chapter 6 generally lead to publications of sufficient quality for a research paper. But the best known of the indexes, the *Readers' Guide to Periodical Literature*, must be used with caution, since most of its periodicals are aimed at popular audiences. Nevertheless, among the 175 periodicals indexed by the *Readers' Guide* are a number that can make a respectable contribution to a serious research paper:

- *The Atlantic* and *Harper's*, monthlies, and *The New Yorker*, a weekly, with substantial articles on world affairs, literature, and the arts;

- *Science, Science News, Scientific American*, and *Aviation Week and Space Technology*, covering developments in science and technology without overpopularizing;

- *Bulletin of the Atomic Scientists*, with serious studies related to the threat of nuclear war;

- *The Nation, The New Republic, The Progressive, Commentary*, and *National Review*, providing political commentary from different ideological perspectives;

- *The New York Review of Books, The New York Times Book Review, The New York Times Magazine*, and *Saturday Review*, offering serious reviews and comment;

- and others like *The Christian Century, Foreign Policy,* and *Vital Speeches of the Day*, whose titles suggest their subject matter.

You will be helped in choosing quality sources by the choices your library has already made. With minor exceptions, college and university libraries get only those books and periodicals suitable for academic research—which is why you may have had to go to the public library to read the latest issue of *Seventeen* or *Home Mechanix*. You are likely to find *The New York Times* in your library, but not *National Enquirer;* you will find the novels of Kate Chopin, but not Harlequin Romances. Somewhere along the line, some librarian or professor decided for each work in your library's collection that it was worth serious scholarly attention.

There are borderline cases, too. Your library will certainly get the newsmagazines—*Time, Newsweek, U.S. News & World Report*. Should you use them as sources? The answer is yes and no. Articles in newsmagazines are like articles in encyclopedias: good for general orientation and overview but often highly condensed. A newsmagazine puts a whole week's worth of news into much less space than a single issue of a daily newspaper. It will offer breadth more often than the depth of coverage that a research paper needs. An exception can be the newsmagazine's cover story, which is often itself a research paper. Though it lacks a list of Works Cited, a cover story will often include interviews with experts doing research in the field, the very persons whose works you would want to cite as sources. Thus a few references to newsmagazines may be appropriate in a research paper, but your paper should not rely principally on them.

Newspapers and Books

Among newspapers, *The New York Times* has attained great respectability and may safely be used as a source for a research paper. Other newspapers with considerable stature include *The Wall Street Journal*, the *Christian Science Monitor*, the *Washington Post,* and the *Los Angeles Times*. The black-and-white, no-comics *New York Times* and *Wall Street Journal* deliberately aim for readers who want in-depth, first-hand coverage of important issues. In contrast, the colorful newspaper *USA Today*, though it has attained the highest circulation in the nation, is more like the quick-answer general sources of the reference room, good for an introduction to a subject but not an in-depth study. As mentioned in an Chapter 3, its editorial page each day provides a wide range of opinion on a given issue. But for your research, even its longer articles are too short to provide the depth your sources should have.

When it comes to books, the question of quality is still more difficult to establish. A university press as publisher is presumption of academic quality, but serious books come from commercial publishers too. Here again your library will be of help. A college or university library will generally not purchase books that are merely popular or recreational. You should be able to use without apology any book your library owns, keeping in mind that not every scholarly book is equally accepted by the academic community and that books sometimes present unorthodox ideas. When possible, use the indexes to find reviews of a book in scholarly journals.

Government Publications

Government publications almost always have sufficient documentary value to warrant use in a research paper—with the understanding that they represent an official point of view. If your library is a U.S. government depository, you will have an abundance of such material on hand. Keep in mind, though, the rule of variety too; no more than two sources of your twelve should come from any one government agency.

Textbooks and Encyclopedias

Although it does have references, one kind of book that is usually not appropriate as a source for a research paper is a textbook. This is because a textbook teaches rather than investigates; it is second-hand rather than first-hand; like a reference work, it offers a broad introduction to an entire field rather than an in-depth study.

Encyclopedias too in most cases are inappropriate sources for a research paper. They are ideal for orienting a researcher to a subject; that is why Chapter 6 made so much of them. But serious research starts where textbooks and encyclopedias leave off.

There are some exceptions to this rule. Occasionally a textbook becomes a classic of scholarship in its own right, like Leonard Bloomfield's *Language* (New York: Holt, 1933) in the field of linguistics. Among encyclopedias, as Chapter 6 mentioned, the *Britannica*'s longer articles—those in the *Macropaedia*—have sufficient scholarly reputation to be appropriate sources for a research paper.

The most important use for textbooks and encyclopedia entries, however, is to point the way. Most of them have references to the books and articles which they use as sources. In turn, you too can look up those references, knowing them to be well regarded by the experts.

A Test of Quality

Gauging quality is always a matter of judgment. There are many factors to consider—publisher, type of publication, intended audience, tone, as well as the subject matter and the author's reputation. But if there is one factor common to sources of good quality, it is their willingness to refer to other serious scholarly sources. A source that cites and lists other sources gives evidence first that it has taken other sources into account, and second that it recognizes that others have important things to say.

By referring to others, a source brings you into the circle of expert discussion of a topic. You not only meet one expert, but are introduced to others. At first you may not understand all that is said, but as you read more you will come to realize what concerns the experts have, what language and approaches they use, where they disagree, and what they all accept as true or reasonable.

LOCATING SOURCES

The next step on the way to the research paper is to find a sufficient quantity of sources that meet the criteria of variety, timeliness, and quality. You will collect entries for them in a *working bibliography*, a list of the sources that you plan to use in your research. If they are sufficiently relevant to your hypothesis, a dozen such sources should be enough to provide you with the evidence to support the final thesis.

The list does have to be open to change. Just as you may have to modify your hypothesis before it becomes your final thesis, so you may need to drop a few of the items in the working bibliography and add others encountered in your reading to come up with the final list of Works Cited for your research paper.

But how can these varied, timely, in-depth, first-hand sources be located? As before, the beginning of the answer lies in the nerve center of the library, the reference room. There you will find the bibliographies and indexes that will lead you to quality sources of in-depth information.

Bibliographies

Consider bibliographies first. Those who write books and articles on the topic of your hypothesis are likely to have their own bibliographies or lists of works cited. So do many of the reference works mentioned in Chapter 6.

The reference room will also have, shelved according to subject, books that are nothing but bibliographies, like the *Cambridge Bibliography of English Literature*.

Especially useful in finding ready-made bibliographies is the periodical known as *Bibliography Index*. With entries arranged by topic, this publication tells you where you can find bibliographies in other books and periodicals. Look at recent issues of *Bibliography Index* and see if you can find an up-to-the-minute bibliography of sources related to your hypothesis. If you can, this stage of your research will proceed quickly. And since the makers of published bibliographies will have been concerned about variety and quality, you can feel reasonably safe in following their lead. They will already have selected what seems most important.

Indexes

The indexes, discussed in the last chapter, contain entries that will allow you to construct your own working bibliography. Your problem usually is choosing from among the many items listed in an index. Look for a review article—*review* in this case meaning a survey and evaluation of studies done by others. Such an article will tell you which studies have been particularly significant and it will give bibliographical references for them.

The abstracting indexes are another way of evaluating potential bibliography items without the effort of locating the actual works. If you find promising summaries in sources like *Biological Abstracts, Sociological*

Abstracts, or *Readers' Guide Abstracts*, for example, you can put the original articles on your working bibliography list. (Getting copies of the unpublished dissertations summarized in *Dissertation Abstracts International*, on the other hand, is more difficult; your instructor may permit you to use the dissertation abstract itself as a source for the research paper.)

Another way to find out about possible sources is through a citation index. This is a publication telling which articles have been cited by authors of subsequent publications. Those articles which are frequently cited will be the most influential.

A citation index also permits you to find out which sources an article has cited. So you can compile a promising bibliography simply by 1) finding a frequently-cited article and 2) noting the sources which that article cites.

There are three citation indexes, covering a wide range of scholarly fields: *Science Citation Index* (published since 1961), *Social Sciences Citation Index* (since 1966), and *Arts and Humanities Citation Index* (since 1977).

Certain single-source indexes may be useful too. *The New York Times Index* leads you only to the pages of the newspaper with "All the News That's Fit to Print," but because it gives exact dates of historical events, government actions, disasters, opening nights of plays, and the like, you can use it as an index to reporting and commentary on those matters in other newspapers, newsmagazines, and journals of opinion.

Many of the indexes are published by the Wilson Company, which also puts out the familiar *Readers' Guide to Periodical Literature*. Regarding quality of sources for a research paper, you need not worry when using the indexes to specialized periodicals in a particular subject like *Art Index, Social Science Index, Education Index*. It is only with the *Readers' Guide* itself that you must exercise caution, staying away from *'Teen* even as you make use of the *Department of State Bulletin*.

Government Publications

If your library is a depository for U.S. government publications, you should not overlook the indexes to them. These include the *Index to U.S. Government Periodicals*, the *Monthly Catalog of United States Government Publications*, and the Government Publishing Office's *Publications Reference File*, known as *PRF*. Also directing to government publications, as well as others, is the index known as *Public Affairs Information Service Bulletin (PAIS)*.

The federal government publishes books, pamphlets, and periodicals that could relate to practically any hypothesis. Here are Works Cited listings for three examples:

Hunger in America: Hearings Before the Subcommittee on Nutrition and
    Investigations of the Committee on Agriculture, Nutrition, and Forestry
    United States Senate, and the Committee on Agriculture, Nutrition, and

Forestry United States Senate. Washington, D.C.: U.S. Government Printing Office, 1988.

Toward Civilization: A Report on Arts Education. Washington, D.C.: National Endowment for the Arts, 1988.

United States Arctic Research Plan: July 1987. Washington, D.C.: Interagency Arctic Research Policy Committee, 1987.

(You will notice that titles of government documents can be long—the better to tell us what's in them.)

Government publications are handled and indexed somewhat differently from other items in your library's collection. Look for guides to the use of government publications, or ask a reference librarian for help.

Obtaining Copies of Sources

The indexes will direct you to sources. You must then find copies of them and examine their contents to see if they do contain material that relates to your hypothesis.

How do you find out whether your library has the source you are looking for? If the source is an article in a periodical, you check your library's list of periodical holdings. This list is likely to be a computer printout, with copies at convenient locations, or a database accessed by a computer terminal.

Books, of course, are indexed in the catalog, which is kept either in alphabetized drawers of 3-by-5 cards or on-line in a computer. The catalog is often the first place to look to see if a library has material on a particular subject, but since any library has only a small fraction of all books published, turning to the catalog before checking the indexes means missing much potential material. Too easily the catalog can become a shortcut, providing you with enough to get by in a paper but causing you to miss other important sources that your library does not happen to have. By concentrating your preliminary search in the reference collection instead, you have learned about all the important materials relating to your hypothesis, not just those materials that can be found in your library.

But the catalog does have value beyond simply telling whether your library has a certain book. Through its subject headings, it tells what else the library has to offer on the subject of your hypothesis. If you know of one book on your topic, you can look under the subject headings that go with the entry for that book to find further books on the same or related topics.

Another useful tool of the catalog is the shelflist. This is simply a listing of all books in the library's collection according to their call numbers, so books on similar topics are grouped together. Looking through the shelflist is like browsing in a section of the bookstacks for other related volumes. The shelflist has the advantage of showing you all the books in the library's collection. If you browse instead in the stacks—which is still a useful exercise—you will be looking at books that are less in demand, ones that have not been checked out.

Other Libraries

Inevitably there will be sources that your library doesn't have budget enough to buy or room enough to shelve. Even if they are not at your library, however, these sources are still available to you through interlibrary loan. In most cases, the loan of a book will be free; an article will come as a photocopy which you may keep, and for which you may have to pay a fee. See your librarian to arrange interlibrary loans, and—because getting material from another library takes time—do it promptly.

If you are in a hurry, you may want to visit other libraries in your neighborhood. Libraries often cooperate with each other in ordering periodicals and expensive books, so that one library in a region will get certain important but less-used works that complement the collection of another library. Your library may have the list of periodicals held by other neighboring libraries, so you won't even have to go there to see if the neighbor has the periodicals you want.

Finally, then, if everything proceeds according to plan, you will start getting the actual books and articles for your research paper. What will you do with them once you have listed them in the working bibliography? You will follow the procedure illustrated in the previous chapter: citing and listing, of course, but above all writing—explaining how the sources provide material that relates to your hypothesis. These processes will be explained in detail starting with Chapter 9.

EXERCISE 7.1—PRIMARY AND SECONDARY SOURCES

Categorize each of the following as a primary or secondary source. Some could be classified either way.

1. Census records of the population of Chicago in 1990.
2. A scholarly article on the people missed by the census in Chicago in 1990.
3. Mayor Daley's statement on the people missed by the census in Chicago in 1990.
4. A biography of Benjamin Franklin by John Updike.
5. The autobiography of Benjamin Franklin.
6. Julius Caesar's history of the Gallic Wars, which he conducted as general of the Roman armies.
7. A modern history of the Gallic Wars.
8. The novel *The Color Purple* by Alice Walker.

9. The film of *The Color Purple* by Steven Spielberg.

10. An article on the novel and film of *The Color Purple* in a scholarly journal.

EXERCISE 7.2—EVALUATING SOURCES

1. Go through a recent issue of a newsmagazine and decide which articles have sufficient depth and first-hand information to be suitable sources for a research paper.

2. Do the same with an issue of *The New York Times* or *The Wall Street Journal.*

3. Discuss the potential of the following as sources of suitable quality for a research paper:

   a. An article in *The World Book Encyclopedia.*

   b. An article in the *Micropaedia* of the *Britannica.*

   c. An article in the *Macropaedia* of the *Britannica.*

   d. A book called *Crazy English: The Ultimate Joy Ride Through Our Language.*

   e. A book called *Historical Change and English Word-Formation.*

   f. A newspaper column by Dr. Lamb on the symptoms and treatment of diverticulosis.

   g. An article in the *New England Journal of Medicine* on the same topic.

   h. A column by Ann Landers with readers' suggestions on how to put an end to the drug problem.

   i. A column in *The Wall Street Journal* by economist Milton Friedman on how to put an end to the drug problem.

   j. An article in an economics journal on how to put an end to the drug problem.

   k. A report from the federal government on how to put an end to the drug problem.

   l. A film review in the student newspaper.

   m. A film review by Siskel and Ebert on television.

   n. A film review by Pauline Kael in *The New Yorker*.

EXERCISE 7.3—THE LIBRARY CATALOG

Start with the catalog listing for a book on the topic of your hypothesis. Use the subject headings included with that listing to find other books on that topic or related topics.

Start with the call number for a book on the topic of your hypothesis. Use the shelflist to find books with similar call numbers on that topic or related topics.

ASSIGNMENT V—WORKING BIBLIOGRAPHY

Locate sources of sufficient quantity, variety, timeliness, and quality that offer material relating to your hypothesis. If your instructor does not specify the number of sources you must have, use the rule of thumb that about a dozen good sources should suffice for a research paper of about 2500 words (8-10 pages). To ensure variety, include both books (for depth and new perspectives) and articles (for immediacy and attention to particular points), and have no more than two items from any one book publisher or periodical. Timeliness requires that at least some of the sources should be recent publications. As for quality, find studies that are addressed to serious scholarly audiences rather than popular treatments aimed at mass audiences.

Compile a working bibliography of your twelve most promising sources. Use the form for the list of Works Cited form exemplified in Chapter 6 and explained further in Chapters 9 and 11. Alphabetize entries according to the first word of each (ignoring *A, An,* and *The*).

Write your research hypothesis before the start of the bibliography.

So that you and your instructor can check for accuracy, provide photocopies of the pages that provide most of the bibliographic information:

—for each *book*, a copy of the title page;

—for each *article in a book*, a copy of the title page of the book plus a copy of the first page of the article;

—for each *article in a journal or magazine*, a copy of the table of contents plus a copy of the first page of the article;

—for each *article in a newspaper*, a copy of the front page showing the masthead plus a copy of the first page of the article.

Label these copies at the top with the first element of the bibliography entry: the author's name or, if no author is given, the title. Arrange the copies in the same order as your bibliography entries, alphabetically by key word, for easy reference.

ALTERNATE ASSIGNMENT V
ANNOTATED WORKING BIBLIOGRAPHY

In addition to the assignment above, your instructor may want you to *annotate* your bibliography: to write a sentence or two following each entry explaining its relevance to your hypothesis. About 50 words is the right length for an annotation. At this stage you need not read the source in its entirety, especially if it is long. Just skim it to see what it contains and write a short summary of how the material will be able to support, oppose, or modify the hypothesis.

A sample page follows for an annotated working bibliography on the hypothesis regarding the monuments of Washington, D.C.

S. Ward
English 202
April 12, 1991

The Monuments of Washington, D.C.

   Hypothesis: The monuments of Washington, D.C. reflect
two American ideals: unity from diversity and the worth of
the individual.

Annotated Working Bibliography

Gallagher, H. M. Pierce. <u>Robert Mills: Architect of the
   Washington Monument 1781-1855</u>. New York: Columbia
   University Press, 1935.
      This chatty biography is written in first-person
   nonacademic style but gives much information about Mills'
   training and views. The author gives her own views on
   the majesty of the Washington Monument and includes a
   composition by a fourteen-year-old boy describing the
   impression it made on him.

Harvey, Frederick L. <u>History of the Washington National
   Monument and Washington National Monument Society</u>.
   Washington: Government Printing Office, 1903. 57th
   Congress, 2d session, Senate Document No. 224.
      Full details of the design and plan of the monument,
   and the accompanying debates, are given in this 362-page
   volume. It includes many documents, including texts of
   orations delivered at the dedication of the monument in
   1885.

<u>Lincoln Memorial: A Guide to the Lincoln Memorial, District
   of Columbia</u>. Produced by the Division of Publications,
   National Park Service. Washington, D.C.: U.S.
   Department of the Interior, 1986.
      Addressed to the general public, this 48-page
   pamphlet gives considerable attention to the ideals
   suggested by Lincoln's life and the monument. The first
   section, for example, by E.J. Applewhite, "places the
   memorial building in the context of Lincoln's position in
   our national consciousness" (2).

Simmons, John K. "Pilgrimage to the Wall." <u>The Christian Century</u> 102 (6 November 1985): 998-999, 1002.

     Simmons brought eighteen students from his class on "Religion and the Impact of the Vietnam War" at the University of California, Santa Barbara across the country to visit the Vietnam Veterans Memorial. Three of the students were Vietnam veterans, and Simmons describes their moving reactions both to the statue of the three soldiers and to the wall with the names of the fallen.

$\triangledown$

CHAPTER EIGHT

MACHINE TOOLS

▽

Use computer databases to make the search for sources more efficient.

(Bibliographic sources are discussed in Chapters 6 and 7. If you have already found sources of sufficient quantity, variety, and quality, proceed to document them [Chapters 9–11] and write about them [Chapters 12–16].)

▽

If a computer database is available to you, use it.

It can shorten the search for sources to the point where you will have an ample supply of in-depth sources in just a few minutes. It can look through many months and years of many indexes in the time it would take you to look through just one year's volume of a printed index.

And it permits you to do things you could not do at all using printed volumes:

You can obtain up-to-the-minute items too new to be in any printed index. You can interact with the computer, broadening the search if you find too few items and narrowing it if you find too many. You can search not only under subject headings, but for key words in titles and abstracts. You can combine several key words and search only for items that use them all. And you can even search for items that use certain key words and *not* certain other ones.

With this speed, convenience, interaction, and the excitement of discovery, the formerly tedious process of looking through printed volumes to compile a list of possible sources has been transformed into an activity that can actually be a pleasure.

One of the pleasures of database searching is that it does not require extensive practice or instruction. You work either with a librarian or directly with a computer terminal. If you do the searching yourself, you will be able to learn by trial and error because the computer is quick and interactive.

This chapter will give a brief overview of the growing world of computer databases and then concentrate on the key to any database search, your mastery of the key words associated with your hypothesis.

A CAUTION ON RANGE AND DEPTH

When you pick up a book, you know it's not the only one in the library. When you enter a computer database, because it contains so much, you may have the impression that it includes everything. But, of course, it doesn't.

Every database is strictly limited. It can give you many citations quickly, but only from a limited range of sources—in fact, often the same range as the printed versions of the indexes. A computer database can contain errors, just as printed ones do. Moreover, databases do not always offer much depth in time. For example, InfoTrac, one of the most accessible of the databases, goes back only three or four years for scholarly journals, and goes back just six months for *The New York Times*. Databases are especially valuable for current and recent information, but for older sources you are likely to have to use print.

By all means, head first for InfoTrac or another computer database when you begin your in-depth research. It will get you off to a fast start. Just remember that it is only a start. You will probably need the help of printed indexes too.

CD-ROM DATABASES

Computer databases come in two kinds: CD-ROM and on-line.

The kind you are most likely to encounter first is CD-ROM, which is short for Compact Disc Read-Only Memory. CD-ROM uses compact discs identical to those designed for stereo music systems. Instead of music, however, each CD-ROM stores many millions of words, which the computer can access in fractions of a second. The disc is inserted in a CD player connected to a personal computer. By following instructions on the computer screen you can conduct your own search of the database.

The amount of information on each CD-ROM disc is equivalent to that contained in whole shelves of books. Dialog, one of the suppliers of CD-ROM databases, figures each disc to be "the equivalent of 1,500 floppy discs, 275,000 pages, 100 million words or 200 pounds of paper!"

CD-ROM indexes are updated frequently, just like printed indexes. Compared to on-line databases, they have the advantage of economy, user-friendliness, and opportunity to explore alternate search strategies without extra charge. If you search an on-line database inefficiently, you pay for the extra time, but with CD searching there is no charge for the connection and you can take all the time you wish.

InfoTrac: Hands On

One collection of CD databases is the InfoTrac system distributed by Information Access Company and available for hands-on user interaction in many libraries. The InfoTrac databases include:

General Periodicals Index. In its Academic Library Edition it indexes 1100 general-interest and scholarly publications in the social and general sciences, humanities, business management, economics, and current affairs. More than 100 of the indexed publications include abstracts. It is updated monthly.

Academic Index. This indexes the most current three or four years of 400 scholarly and general interest journals in the humanities, social sciences, general sciences, and current events. It also covers the last six months of *The New York Times*. It is updated monthly.

Government Publications Index. An index to the *Monthly Catalog* of the U. S. Government Printing Office, with coverage since 1976.

Health Index. An index to 100 publications on health, fitness, and nutrition, including professional journals but also consumer-oriented magazines, newsletters, and health-related articles from over 2500 magazines and newspapers. Coverage begins in 1988 and for some publications goes back to 1977. It is updated monthly.

LegalTrac. This indexes over 800 legal publications, including all major law reviews, seven legal newspapers, and bar association journals. Coverage begins 1980. It is updated monthly.

National Newspaper Index. This provides an index to *The New York Times, The Wall Street Journal*, the *Christian Science Monitor*, the *Washington Post*, and the *Los Angeles Times* for the last three or four years. It is updated monthly.

The H. W. Wilson Company, publisher of the *Readers' Guide to Periodical Literature* and many other printed indexes, is also a leader in CD publishing. Wilson offers more than two dozen CD indexes, including

Applied Science and Technology Index

Art Index

Book Review Digest

Business Periodicals Index

Education Index

Essay and General Literature Index

Film Literature Index

General Science Index

Government Publications Office Monthly Catalog

Humanities Index

Index to Legal Periodicals

Index to U.S. Government Periodicals

MLA International Bibliography

Readers' Guide Abstracts

Readers' Guide to Periodical Literature

Social Sciences Index

Most of the Wilson indexes are updated four times a year.

University Microfilms International, publisher of periodicals in microfilm and microfiche, offers Newspaper Abstracts Ondisc (indexing eight newspapers), Periodical Abstracts Ondisc (indexing over 300 general-reference periodicals), and Resource/One (indexing 130 general-interest periodicals and highlights of *The New York Times*).

Many specialized works are on CD as well. *The Oxford English Dictionary* is available on disc (though in its first edition, not its second), as are complete texts of the Bible and the works of Shakespeare. Bibliographies of books published in earlier centuries are available on the CD-ROM Eighteenth-Century Short Title Catalogue and North American Imprints Program. Even the Thesaurus Linguae Graecae, a database of all of the texts in the ancient Greek language from the time of Homer (about 750 B.C.) to 600 A.D., is available on CD.

ON-LINE DATABASES

If a CD-ROM database contains the equivalent of a shelf of printed indexes, the on-line services can hold as much as a whole reference room. They are accordingly more expensive and difficult to use. Most likely you will not be able to access them yourself but will work with a reference librarian, because with on-line databases every second of access costs money. The on-line databases are collections of millions of items and billions of words at a central location. You connect with them by modem and telephone line and pay for the time you use.

"The World's Largest Online Knowledgebank" is Dialog, headquartered in Palo Alto, California. A typical online search, says Dialog, takes about five to ten minutes and averages about $2 per minute. As of December 1989, Dialog had over 150 million records in over 350 different databases. Among the 350 databases are these indexes and abstracts:

Biography Master Index

Book Review Index

ERIC Resources in Education

Monthly Catalog of United States Government Publications

Magazine Index

Modern Language Association Bibliography

National Newspaper Index

Nursing and Allied Health Index

Philosopher's Index

Religion Index

Arts and Humanities Citation Index

Science Citation Index

Social Sciences Citation Index

Chemical Abstracts

Congressional Record Abstracts

Dissertation Abstracts

Historical Abstracts

Linguistics and Language Behavior Abstracts

Mental Health Abstracts

Pollution Abstracts

U.S. Patents Abstracts

In addition, Dialog offers the full text of reference works and news media:

Academic American Encyclopedia

Associated Press News

The Bible, King James Version

Facts on File

Jane's Defense and Aerospace News / Analysis

Medline (U.S. National Library of Medicine)

United Press International News

Washington Post

Who's Who in America

In fact, Dialog contains the complete text of nearly 500 journals and newspapers, plus up-to-the-minute news and press releases.

A search strategy for Dialog involves specifying not only your key words but also which of the 350 databases you want to search (doing them all can be expensive and can overwhelm you with information) along with the time limits you wish for the citations. You can get a printed record of the bibliographic items, abstracts, and texts obtained by your search.

Another source of on-line databases is the H. W. Wilson Company. All of the indexes listed above as available on CD from Wilson are available on "Wilsonline" too.

And there are other on-line databases as well. Two of the most notable are Lexis, which provides legal citations, and Nexis, which has the full text of hundreds of magazines, journals, and newspapers.

SEARCH STRATEGIES

Whatever your database, and whether on-line or CD-ROM, you will be asked to provide key words for a search to locate relevant items within the equivalent of thousands or millions of pages. This is where your efforts in developing key words from *Library of Congress Subject Headings* and your reading become especially important.

As with your search through printed indexes, you can search under each of your key words. But the computer permits more complex searching, using combinations of key words in various ways. One method of combination is known as Boolean logic. It involves three terms:

AND—combining two key words so that the computer will seek only those items that use both.

OR—combining two key words so that the computer will seek all items that use either one or both.

AND NOT—combining two key words so that the computer will seek all items containing the first provided they do not contain the second.

This logic allows combinations like:

"Berlin Wall" AND "Communism"

"Sumo" AND NOT "Japan" (for Sumo wrestling elsewhere in the world)

"Television" AND "Teenagers" AND NOT "Commercials"

"Nested" combinations may also be possible, such as:

"Insurance" AND ("Term" OR "Whole life")

which would find information on two kinds of life insurance, either term or whole life, but would leave out insurance on cars or homes.

The best combination in each case must be determined by actual investigation. If you get too many items, you can narrow your search by adding another AND term; if you get too few, you can try OR.

The computer will not necessarily ask for this format. It may simply ask you for one key word, then another; and it may ask you separately about authors, titles, databases, and dates. One program, for example, invites you to narrow your search by specifying whether your key word is a topic, person, organization, or geographical area.

Some programs will search just the subject headings assigned to a bibliography entry; others will search every word of text in the database, including abstracts, to let you know if your key words are present.

Whatever the format, you will be able to get a printed copy of the entries you wish to use. This is one final advantage in speed and efficiency for the computer database. Not only is it much faster to let the computer print the entry you want, instead of hand copying it, but also it guarantees accuracy; it will not make a mistake in copying. The drawback is that taking notes by hand forces you to think about the entries you are making and to choose only ones that will be worth the effort. In contrast, it is so easy to extract sources from a computer that you may be tempted to put too many on your list. Look the list over carefully, because when it comes to working with sources, there still is no substitute for alert reading and serious thinking about them.

EXERCISE 8.1—KEY WORDS AND BOOLEAN LOGIC

Consider what key words to use, in what combination, in a computer search to find sources for the following hypotheses. Consult *Library of Congress Subject Headings* for assistance. Also choose which one of the databases mentioned in this chapter you would search first.

After you have developed a search strategy for one of these hypotheses, try it out on a computer database to which you have access.

1. Dreams are essential for mental health. (See Chapter 5.)
2. Athletic training improves body responses. (See Chapter 5.)
3. The Panama Canal has hindered the development of democracy in Panama.
4. Vladimir Nabokov's novels were strongly influenced by his residing in five countries: Russia, England, Germany, France, and the United States.
5. Prices of modern paintings and sculpture have increased at recent auctions.
6. Events in Eastern Europe brought the Cold War to an end in 1989.
7. Eating broccoli helps prevent cancer of the gastrointestinal tract.
8. Television watching weakens the academic performance of high school students.
9. The trumpeter swan is an endangered species.
10. The United States has had a generally positive relationship with China.

ASSIGNMENT VI—COMPUTER SEARCH FOR SOURCES

If you have access to a computer database, devise a search strategy for your research hypothesis as in the preceding exercise and try it out on the database. Use the results of the search to modify your strategy as necessary so that it will obtain a dozen sources of appropriate variety, timeliness, and quality.

$\triangledown$

PART III:

Listing and Citing Sources

▽

CHAPTER NINE

LISTING WORKS

▽

For each source you use, list full publication information in a list of Works Cited. Choose from three basic forms.

(Sources for the research paper are discussed in Chapters 7 and 8. After you have listed the Works Cited entry for a source, proceed to write about the evidence that the source provides for your hypothesis [Chapters 12–16].)

▽

Whether you use words or just ideas from a source, it must appear in the list of Works Cited at the end of the paper. There are three good reasons for listing sources. The first is simply to give credit where credit is due. If you have borrowed ideas, information, or words from a source, you must let your reader know. Failure to do so makes it appear that the material is yours, and that false appearance is plagiarism.

A second and more positive reason to list sources is that they add credibility to a research paper. If you have chosen sources of high quality, that quality will transfer to your paper along with the material of your sources. If the sources are authoritative, the paper will be.

And a third reason to list them is to let the reader know where to get more information. Your paper may stimulate the reader to pay you the compliment of wanting to find out more about the subject.

So providing information about your sources is an important function of the research paper. This information is assembled in an alphabetical list of Works Cited at the end of your paper. (In the text of the paper you cite the work by brief reference to the author and page number. This was illustrated in Chapter 6 and will be explained more fully in Chapter 10.)

The rules for listing the information for a Works Cited entry may seem arbitrary, but they have all evolved from the actual practice of researchers, and they have the practical purpose of providing your reader with information quickly and efficiently. The essentials of a system of listing and citing derived from that recommended by the Modern Language Association of America

(MLA) will be described in this chapter. Further details of MLA style, and an explanation of the closely-related American Psychological Association (APA) style used in the social sciences, will be available in Chapter 11.

WHEN AND WHERE TO LIST

Even though it appears last in your research paper, the listing should be the first thing you write when you have discovered a relevant source. If you wait to list the work until you have put the source away, you are likely to find some necessary bibliographical fact missing from your notes. Avoiding this misfortune is easy if you prepare a Works Cited listing each time you open a book or periodical and decide to use it.

Where do you write it down? The traditional method has been to use 3-by-5-inch index cards, one for each source. When you have made entries for all your sources, you alphabetize them according to the first word of each entry and type them in a list. Another way is to use a sheet of paper, or a form like the ones in Appendix II. That has the advantage of keeping the listing with the notes you have written about that source; it has the disadvantage of requiring extra work if you have more than one set of notes about a given source. If you are using a word processor or computer to write your research paper, a third method is to type each listing into a special Works Cited file as you go along. Some computer software programs will automatically put bibliographic information into a standard form. If you have that software, select MLA style—the style we are following here, in a simplified version and with fewer abbreviations.

THREE BASIC FORMS

Wherever you write it, the Works Cited listing will take one of three basic forms, depending on whether it is an entire book, an article in a book, or an article in a periodical. These are the forms, with examples for each:

1. Entire Book

Information needed

```
Last Name of Author, First Name or Names.  Title of Book.
     Edited by Name of Editor of Book.  Edition of Book.
     Volume(s) used.  City, State of Publication: Name of
     Publishing Company, Year of Publication.
```

Example

```
Rosenberg, Bruce A.  Custer and the Epic of Defeat.
     University Park, Pennsylvania:  Pennsylvania State
     University Press, 1974.
```

2. Article in Book

Information needed

```
Last Name of Author, First Name or Names.  "Title of
    Article."  Book in Which Article Is Found.  Edited
    by Name of Editor of Book.  Edition of Book.  City,
    State of Publication: Name of Publishing Company,
    Year of Publication.  Volume number:  Pages on which
    article is found.
```

Example

```
Garcia, Ofelia.  "Bilingualism in the United States:
    Present Attitudes in the Light of Past Policies."
    The English Language Today.  Edited by Sidney
    Greenbaum.  Oxford, England: Pergamon Institute of
    English, 1985.  147-158.
```

3. Article in Periodical

Information needed

```
Last Name of Author, First Name or Names.  "Title of
    Article."  Title of Periodical Volume number (Day
    Month Year): Pages on which article is found.
```

Example

```
Miller, Keith D.  "Composing Martin Luther King, Jr."
    PMLA 105 (January 1990): 70-82.
```

That is all there is to it: Match your source to the right form and provide the requisite information. If you can do this, there is no need to read further in this chapter. You can go on to the simple rules for citing (Chapter 10) and then concentrate on the central activity of research, the activity that should have your greatest attention—the actual writing about sources (Chapters 12–14).

Further explanations, however, may be called for, particularly in cases that do not exactly follow the three basic patterns. The rest of this chapter explains how to choose the right form; what information goes into each form, in what order; and where to find the information. Examples of forms for special circumstances are in Chapter 11.

CHOOSING THE RIGHT FORM

You must distinguish among book, article in book, and article in periodical in order to choose the appropriate form for a Works Cited listing.

The first distinction is between *book* and *periodical*. How do you know which is which? A book is a one-time publication, while a periodical keeps coming. A book may be reprinted in a new edition, but its contents remain basically the same. A periodical, in contrast, is published again and again with the same title but different contents.

There are also other, less significant indications of the difference. Each book looks different; each issue of a periodical looks approximately the same. Your library buys a book, but subscribes to a periodical.

To take examples: E. D. Hirsch, Jr.'s *Cultural Literacy: What Every American Needs to Know* (Boston: Houghton Mifflin Company, 1987) is a book; *Scientific American* is a periodical. Charles Whited's *Knight: A Publisher in the Tumultuous Century* (New York: Dutton, 1988) is a book; *The New York Times* is a periodical.

The distinction between book and periodical is usually not too hard to make. But if you have a book in your hands, you are faced with a more difficult choice: Is your source to be treated as *article in book* or just as a plain *book*?

The answer to this question depends on the kind of book it is. If one author, or one group of authors, has written the entire book, you list it according to the pattern for a book. But if different authors have written different parts of the book, you must list your source as article in book.

It is easy to overlook separate authorship of separate parts. To find out, look on the title page. If the title page gives an author's name (or the names of several authors), perhaps with the word "By," then the entire book is by a single author or group of authors and should probably be treated as a book. But if it says "Edited by" or "Editor," that is a strong indication that the different parts will be by different people, and you should treat your particular source as article in book.

If the title page gives no names at all, neither authors nor editors, then turn to the table of contents. If the individual parts are by separate authors, their names will be with those parts in the table of contents. That means listing your source as article in book.

Finally, look inside the book at the actual contents. Is it a book that you would normally start reading at the beginning and continue to the end? If so, and if the parts are not by separate authors, list it as a book. Both *Cultural Literacy* and *Knight* are like that.

But would you instead expect to turn to a specific part and read that, regardless of what comes before or after? Then you have an article in a book. Encyclopedias, dictionaries, and most reference works are like that. So are anthologies and proceedings of conferences.

Authors versus Editors

The difference between authors and editors needs to be clear. An author is the one who writes the material. An editor is someone who takes the work of authors and presents it—collecting, revising, or commenting on the work of others. The author is the most important and is named first in all three kinds of listings.

How can you tell an author from an editor? You presume that, unless stated otherwise, a name given with a source indicates an author. At the start or end of an article, or on the title page of a book, a name by itself or with the word "By" is presumed to be the name of an author. An editor, on the other hand, will be identified by the words "Editor" or "Edited by." The same holds true for your Works Cited listing. A name alone (usually at the start of the listing) is presumed to be the author; if you name an editor, put *Edited by* in front of the name.

Fitting the Categories

Every source you use will fit in one of the three categories, even if you use something that is not a book or article. For example:

- Pamphlets, manuscripts, dissertations, unpublished letters, computer printouts, lectures, oral interviews, paintings, musical compositions, motion pictures, television programs, and videotapes all usually have the same author or authors, and are not items in a collection, so they are treated like books (category 1).

- Poems, stories, and speeches in collections all usually have separate authors and thus are treated like articles in books (category 2).

- Laws and court decisions in legal volumes have separate authors and thus are treated like articles in books (category 2).

- Songs or musical numbers on tapes or compact disks, if they are only part of what is on the tape or disk, are treated like articles in books (category 2). Complete albums, tapes, or disks are treated like books (category 1).

- Photographs in books usually have separate photographers and thus are treated like articles in books (category 2); photographs in magazines and newspapers have separate photographers and thus are treated like articles in periodicals (category 3).

- Poems and stories, reviews, interviews, texts of speeches in magazines and newspapers all usually have separate authors and thus are treated like articles in periodicals (category 3).

- Articles or entries in computer databases are treated like articles in periodicals (category 3).

In short, just about anything you can use as a source will fit one of the three models. But most of the time your choice will not be so complicated; you will be using standard library materials, that is, books and periodicals. Let us now look at each in turn.

THE FIRST BASIC FORM: BOOK

When your source is a book entirely by one author or by one group of authors, the Works Cited listing uses this information:

- *Author's name* (last name first), exactly as given on title page, but *without* personal titles (Dr., The Honorable) or degrees (M.D., Ph.D.), and using regular capitalization of the first letters only.
- *Title of book* (underlined), exactly as given on the title page, using a colon (:) to separate the title from the subtitle, if any; using regular capitalization of the first letters only.
- *Editor's name*, if given.
- *Edition of book* (first, second, etc.), if given.
- *Volume number(s)* of the volume used, if the source has more than one volume.
- *City and state of publication*, as given on the title page. If more than one city and state are given, you need to record only the first.
- *Name of publishing company*, as given on the title page. If more than one publisher is given, you need to record only the first.
- *Year of publication*, the latest copyright year, given on the front or back of the title page.

An asterisk (*) indicates information that is not always available. If it is available, include it; if not, omit it and continue the entry.

You obtain this information from the book itself, to ensure accuracy, rather than from indexes or the library catalog. All of the needed information will be found in one place: on the front and back of the title page.

The entry follows this format:

```
                (Entire book by same author)
Last Name of Author, First Name or Names.   Title of Book.
     Edited by Name of Editor of Book.   Edition of Book.
     Volume used.   City, State of Publication: Name of
     Publishing Company, Year of Publication.
```

Here, for example, is the entry for the volume by Talbot Faulkner Hamlin whose title page is shown in Figure 9-1. Notice that there is no editor, edition, or volume number, and that only the first city and publisher are mentioned.

```
Hamlin, Talbot Faulkner.   The American Spirit in
     Architecture.   New Haven: Yale University Press,
     1926.
```

Two Authors

If a work has two authors, list them both, with a comma in between. Only the first of the names goes in reverse order—for example, *Kerrigan, William J.*—because that last name is used to lead the reader from your text to your list of Works Cited and is also used to alphabetize the entry in the list of

THE PAGEANT OF AMERICA

THE
AMERICAN SPIRIT
IN ARCHITECTURE

BY

TALBOT FAULKNER HAMLIN

NEW HAVEN · YALE UNIVERSITY PRESS
TORONTO · GLASGOW, BROOK & CO.
LONDON HUMPHREY MILFORD
OXFORD UNIVERSITY PRESS

1926

Figure 9-1

Works Cited. The second name goes in the usual order—for example, *Frederic G. Cassidy*. Sources generally give names in order of importance, so be sure to follow the same order as the source. For example:

```
Freidel, Frank, and Lonnelle Aikman.  George Washington:
     Man and Monument.  Washington, D.C.: Washington
     National Monument Association, 1965.
```

Three or More Authors

Few books have more than two authors—unless you are dealing with articles in books, which are a different category. But if you do find a book written in its entirety by three or more authors, name all of them. Again, only the first of the names goes in reverse order. Separate the names by commas. The last two names are joined by *and*. For example:

```
Quirk, Randolph, Sidney Greenbaum, Geoffrey Leech, and
     Jan Svartvik.  A Comprehensive Grammar of the
     English Language.  London: Longman, 1985.
```

No Author

Sometimes the author will not be named on the title page or elsewhere in the book. In that case, skip the place for author and simply begin the listing with the title, as in the following example.

```
Lincoln Memorial: A Guide to the Lincoln Memorial,
     District of Columbia.  Washington, D.C.: U.S.
     Department of the Interior, 1986.
```

Including Information

When in doubt, include information rather than leaving it out. For example, the subtitle (a second title that appears on the title page, like *Writing the Research Paper* for this book) is not strictly necessary to identify a book or article, but it usually helps explain the content. Consider a book with the title *Zion in the Courts*. What might that be about? The subtitle makes it clear: *A Legal History of the Church of Jesus Christ of Latter-day Saints, 1830-1900*. Or consider how necessary for explanation the subtitle is in *World Population Crisis: The United States Response*.

Likewise, an author's full name will help avoid confusion with other authors. Even the full name of the publisher helps avoid misreading, although strict MLA style calls for abbreviation of publishers' names, as Chapter 11 will explain.

If you happen to provide more information than is strictly necessary, no harm is done. For example, you may happen to copy from a title page certain

identifying information about an author, like the degree M.D. This is information we customarily do not bother to put in our bibliographies; all authors,
no matter how degreed or titled, go by their plain names in a list of Works
Cited. But it does not misinform the reader if you happen to add the M.D.

Or, to take another example, you may find yourself listing not just the first
of the cities and publishers named on the title page, but all of them: New
Haven: Yale University Press, Toronto: Glasgow, Brook & Co., and London:
Humphrey Milford, Oxford University Press, to take the example of Hamlin's
book. While listing more than one pair is not customary, there is no harm in
mentioning more, except that it takes up space. Your instructor can ask you
to remove the extra publication data when you compile your final list of
Works Cited. When in doubt, include information.

Extra Information

Some extra information is not only permissible but highly desirable if your
Works Cited entry is to guide the reader to the exact source you used. For
example, the guidebook to the Lincoln Memorial cited earlier is listed on its
title page as "produced" by a government agency. That is not the same as
author or title, but it might help someone locate a copy. So it would be helpful
to include the extra information, putting it at the end of the entry if there is
no natural place for it earlier:

```
Lincoln Memorial: A Guide to the Lincoln Memorial,
     District of Columbia.  Washington, D.C.: U.S.
     Department of the Interior, 1986.  Produced by the
     Division of Publications, National Park Service.
```

Other extra information includes a book's membership in a series or its
status as a reprint of a book published years earlier.

THE SECOND BASIC FORM:
ARTICLE IN BOOK

An article in a book requires the same kind of entry as the entire book, but
with something added at the beginning and the end. The addition at the
beginning is the author and title of the article; the addition at the end is the
page numbers indicating the range of pages that the article occupies. Also,
the volume number, if any, appears at the end with the page number, instead
of in the middle.

This is the information you need:

- *Author's name* (last name first), exactly as given at the start or
  end of the article, without personal titles (Dr., The Honorable) or
  degrees (M.D., Ph.D.), and using regular capitalization of the first
  letters only.

- *Title of article* (in quotation marks), exactly as given at the start of the article, using a colon (:) to separate the title from the subtitle, if any; using regular capitalization of the first letters only.
- *Title of book* (underlined), exactly as given on the title page.
- **Editor's name*, if given.
- **Edition of book* (first, second, etc.), if given.
- *City and state of publication*, as given on the title page. If more than one city and state are given, you need to record only the first.
- *Name of publishing company*, as given on the title page. If more than one publisher is given, you need to record only the first.
- *Year of publication*, the latest copyright year, given on the front or back of the title page.
- **Volume number* of the volume in which the article is found, if the source has more than one volume.
- *Page numbers* of the pages on which the article begins and ends.

As before, an asterisk (*) indicates information that is not always available. If it is available, include it; if not, omit it and continue the entry.

Here is the information arranged and punctuated for the list of Works Cited.

```
                    (Article in book)
Last Name of Author, First Name or Names.  "Title of
     Article."  Book in Which Article Is Found.  Edited
     by Name of Editor of Book.  Edition of Book.  City,
     State of Publication: Name of Publishing Company,
     Year of Publication.  Volume number:  Pages on which
     article is found.
```

Here is an example of an article in a collection of essays:

```
Walker, Alice.  "Beauty: When the Other Dancer Is the
     Self."  Modern American Prose: Fifteen Writers.
     Edited by John Clifford and Robert DiYanni.  2nd
     edition.  New York: Random House, 1987.  443-450.
```

The same rules as before apply regarding multiple authors (put last name before first only when it is the first item in the entry) and regarding subtitles (include them) and inclusiveness in general. The principle of inclusiveness suggests that we add something to the Alice Walker listing to let the reader know that her essay was published earlier. In the back of the Clifford and DiYanni book is the copyright notice saying it is "from *In Search of Our Mothers' Gardens* by Alice Walker. Copyright © 1983 by Alice Walker." That is not enough to provide full bibliographic information, but a short note could be added to the end of the entry:

```
Walker, Alice.   "Beauty: When the Other Dancer Is the
     Self."  Modern American Prose: Fifteen Writers.
     Edited by John Clifford and Robert DiYanni.  2nd
     edition.  New York: Random House, 1987.  443-450.
     Originally published 1983.
```

THE THIRD BASIC FORM: ARTICLE IN PERIODICAL

The third and last of the basic forms for Works Cited entries is for an article in a periodical—a magazine, journal, or newspaper which is published repeatedly with the same title but with different contents and different dates and volume numbers. *The New Yorker, Time*, and *Consumer Reports* are all examples of magazines, aimed at general audiences; *Language* and the *American Historical Review* are examples of what we call journals, aimed at scholars and scientists, specialists in academic fields of study; *The Wall Street Journal, The New York Times,* and your hometown paper are examples of newspapers. All are periodicals, and we treat articles in all periodicals the same way.

The entry for an article in a periodical has the same beginning and end as the entry for an article in a book: author and title of article, beginning and ending page numbers. In the middle comes different information, suited to the different nature of a periodical. Information about place and publisher is not necessary, but it is important to have the volume number and the exact date. This is the required information:

- *Author's name* (last name first), exactly as given at the start or end of the article, without personal titles (Dr., The Honorable) or degrees (M.D., Ph.D.), and using regular capitalization of the first letters only.

- *Title of article* (in quotation marks), exactly as given at the start of the article, using a colon (:) to separate the title from the subtitle, if any; using regular capitalization of the first letters only.

- *Title of periodical* (underlined), exactly as given in the table of contents, using a colon (:) to separate the title from the subtitle, if any; using regular capitalization of the first letters only.

- *Volume number* of the issue in which the article is found.

- *Exact date of that issue* (day, month, year).

- *Page numbers* of the pages on which the entire article is found.

Again an asterisk (*) indicates information that is not always available. The volume number is one of those items. For scholarly journals, which number their pages consecutively through an entire volume, the volume number is prominent and important. For newspapers and popular magazines, which start numbering anew with each issue, the volume number is less important. MLA style allows the volume number to be omitted for those publications.

This is the format for the information:

```
                  (Article in periodical)
Last Name of Author, First Name or Names.  "Title of
     Article."  Title of Periodical Volume number (Day
     Month Year): Pages on which article is found.
```

Here is an example for an article in a scholarly journal:

```
Clark, Thomas L.  "Cheating Terms in Cards and Dice."
     American Speech 61 (Spring 1986): 3-32.
```

If no author is named, simply begin with the title of the article, as in the case of a book that has no author named.

```
"Kissinger vs. Nixon."  Time 134 (25 December 1989): 32.
```

List All the Pages of an Article

The entry for an article in a periodical, like that for an article in a book, should list all of the pages on which the article is found so that a reader of the list of Works Cited will know how long the article is and will be able to specify the exact pages in ordering a copy. Sometimes an article skips pages, as in this example:

```
Simmons, John K.  "Pilgrimage to the Wall."  The
     Christian Century 102 (6 November 1985): 998-999,
     1002.
```

Here the numbers at the end indicate that the article is to be found on pages 998 through 999 and also on page 1002.

A newspaper article is treated much like articles in other periodicals, using headlines and subheads for titles and subtitles. For example:

```
Waldman, Peter.  "Tobacco Firms Try Soft, Feminine Sell:
     But in Targeting Women, They Spark Backlash."  The
     Wall Street Journal 71 (19 December 1989): B1, B8.
```

At the end of the entry "B1, B8" means the article started on page B1 and ended on page B8.

This completes our review of the three basic forms for listing works. The point is not to become entangled in details but to ensure that the listing gives the reader enough information to be able to locate a copy of the exact source you used in any library that has it.

A list of Works Cited means nothing unless the works are cited, so that is the subject of the next chapter.

EXERCISE 9.1—LISTING WORKS

For each of the items below, determine whether it is a book, an article in a book, or an article in a periodical. Then using the appropriate basic form, write a Works Cited entry for it.

1. In 1990 the sixth edition of *Writing Research Papers: A Complete Guide* was published by Scott, Foresman/Little, Brown Higher Education. That is a division of Scott, Foresman and Company in Glenview, Illinois. The author is James D. Lester of Austin Peay State University.

2. The January 1990 *National Geographic* has an article by Jon Thompson called "Inside the Kremlin." It runs from pages 62 through 80 and then is continued on 93 through 105. The issue is Vol. 177, No. 1.

3. An article called "Taxes" in *The World Almanac and Book of Facts 1990* runs from pages 109 through 118. Mark S. Hoffman is the editor of the book, but no author is named for the article. The *Almanac* itself was published in New York in 1989 by the publisher World Almanac.

4. *The Tragedy of King Lear* by William Shakespeare has been edited by Russell Fraser. With new dramatic criticism and an updated bibliography, it was published by New American Library in New York. The latest copyright date was 1987.

5. An article in *The Wall Street Journal* of December 21, 1989 is headlined "Turning 50 Now Means Some Skin Off Rudolph's Nose," with a subhead "Most Famous Reindeer of All Gets a Facelift for the '90s; He Almost Became Rollo." The author is Carrie Dolan. The article starts on the front page, page A1, and is continued on page A10. The issue is Vol. LXXI, No. 48.

6. Raymond Bonner reports on the September 1989 election in South Africa in an article titled "A Reporter at Large: Choices" in the December 25, 1989 issue of *The New Yorker*. It is Volume 65, No. 45. The article is on pages 43 through 69.

7. The Northwestern University Press, in Evanston, Illinois, in 1969 published a book by Richard E. Palmer called *Hermeneutics*. Its subtitle is *Interpretation Theory in Schleiermacher, Dilthey, Heidegger, and Gadamer*. It is one of the Northwestern University Studies in Phenomenology and Existential Philosophy.

8. Karen Adams and Carole Edelsky wrote a piece called "Male and Female Styles in Political Debates." It was published in 1988 by the University of Texas, Department of Linguistics, Austin, Texas. You will find it on pages 18-24 in a volume called *Linguistic Change & Contact,* with editors Kathleen Ferrara, Becky Brown, Keith Walters, and John Baugh. This was the Proceedings of the Sixteenth Annual Conference on New Ways of Analyzing Variation.

ASSIGNMENT VII—DOCUMENTATION

Whenever you find a source relevant to your thesis, determine which of the three basic forms it fits and write a Works Cited entry for it. Then if you later decide to cite the source in your paper, you will not have to go back for further information. You may use the worksheets in Appendix II.

$\triangledown$

CHAPTER TEN

CITING WORKS

▽

In the text of your paper, cite the author and state the page each time you use a source.

(On writing sentences that relate the source to the hypothesis, see Chapters 12 through 16. Instructions for listing Works Cited are in Chapters 9 and 11.)

▽

This chapter can be brief because the rule for citing sources is much simpler than the footnote system which it replaced. The rule is this: Every time you write about a source, you *cite* it. That is, you name the author and tell which page or pages you are using. Do this *in the first sentence* that uses a source; if there is more than one sentence, put the page number also at the end of the last sentence using the source and at the end of any sentence when the reference changes to another page.

You do this whenever you make use of information from a source, *even when you do not use the words of the source.* (Using words from the source is the subject of the chapter on quotation, Chapter 14.)

Naming the author has three purposes. First, it lets your reader know where your information comes from and who is responsible for it. Second, it directs your reader to the list of Works Cited, if the reader wishes to know more about the source or obtain a copy of it. Third, it tells your reader when you have begun to use a source, something that is especially important when you are not otherwise indicating it by putting material in quotation marks. (The last page number in parentheses tells when you have finished.)

To illustrate the process of citation, let us refer to one of the works listed in Chapter 9. A sentence discussing the work—and citing it—is followed by the listing to which the citation refers. (In the final research paper, the list of Works Cited will be on a separate last page, alphabetically arranged.)

> Thomas L. Clark states that very few of the terms
> for cheating in gambling have been recorded in historical
> dictionaries (6).

Works Cited

> Clark, Thomas L.   "Cheating Terms in Cards and Dice."
>   <u>American Speech</u> 61 (Spring 1986): 3-32.

This is a simple example. The sentence begins with the name of the author, thus notifying your reader that you are beginning to use material from a source. The exact page that provides the material is the number in parentheses at the end of the sentence. The Works Cited listing, on the other hand, gives the full range of pages of the article.

Here is another example:

> Talbot Faulkner Hamlin, in his 1926 survey <u>The
> American Spirit in Architecture</u>, observes that the
> simplicity and plainness of the Washington Monument lend
> it power and authority (225).

Works Cited

> Hamlin, Talbot Faulkner. <u>The American Spirit in
>   Architecture</u>. New Haven: Yale University Press, 1926.

Again the sentence signals the beginning of the use of a source by naming the author and ends with the specific page number in parentheses. This sentence also has further information about the source—its title and date. Stating title and date is optional when you cite a source, but you may want to mention one or the other to give your reader an idea of the kind of source you are using. It is always appropriate to name a newspaper, for example:

> <u>The Wall Street Journal</u> reports that cigarette
> advertising targeted at women has itself been the target
> of protests by women's groups (Waldman B1).

Works Cited

> Waldman, Peter.   "Tobacco Firms Try Soft, Feminine Sell:
>   But in Targeting Women, They Spark Backlash."   <u>The
>   Wall Street Journal</u> 71 (19 December 1989): B1, B8.

In this example, the name of the source rather than the author's name begins the sentence. It is still necessary to cite the author's last name in order to lead the reader to the right Works Cited listing, so that name is put in parentheses with the page number at the end of the sentence.

CITING WITHOUT AN AUTHOR

If no author is indicated for a source, the title must be mentioned in the sentences discussing it, because in that case the title comes first in the list of Works Cited:

> <u>The New Encyclopaedia Britannica</u> notes that the
> Jefferson Memorial is located not in an urban environment
> but in an 18-acre park, further set off by the cherry trees
> of the Tidal Basin which bloom in the spring ("Jefferson
> Memorial" 523). Also emphasizing support for individual
> independence is the depiction on the monument of Jefferson
> working on the Declaration of Independence (523).
>
> Works Cited
>
> "Jefferson Memorial."   <u>The New Encyclopaedia Britannica</u>.
>   15th edition. Chicago: Encyclopaedia Britannica,
>   Inc., 1987. 6: 523.

This example illustrates another principle of citation: If you have more than one sentence making use of a source, you indicate the page number at the end of the first such sentence and also at the end of the last. The repetition of the page number at the end of the last sentence signals the reader that you have finished your reference to the source.

CHANGING PAGES

What if you use material from different pages? You put the new page number in parentheses at the end of the first sentence making use of that page.

> According to Richard Palmer, the earliest of the
> modern definitions of hermeneutics is that it is a method
> of biblical interpretation (34). A second definition
> considers hermeneutics to be the grammatical and
> historical investigation of biblical texts (38).
>
> Works Cited
>
> Palmer, Richard E. <u>Hermeneutics: Interpretation Theory</u>
>   <u>in Schleiermacher, Dilthey, Heidegger, and Gadamer</u>.
>   Evanston: Northwestern University Press, 1969.

PROPER INTRODUCTIONS

The sentence naming the author and introducing the borrowed material provides an opportunity to explain exactly what kind of material it is through the choice of verb or other connecting words. Most often you will use facts or information from a source, and if so, your introduction can make that clear:

According to (Author), ...

(Author) states that. . . .

(Author) says. . . .

(Author) reports that. . . .

As (Author) states, ...

As (Author) says, . . .

As (Author) reports, ...

It is reported by (Author) that. . . .

Sometimes, however, you will be reporting an author's reasoning, explanation, argument or conclusion. The word you choose to introduce the author's material should reflect its nature:

(Author) reasons that. . . .

(Author) explains that. . . .

(Author) argues that. . . .

(Author) concludes that. . . .

(Author) emphasizes that. . . .

(Author) denies that. . . .

(Author) speculates that. . . .

(Author) proposes that. . . .

(Author) hopes that. . . .

(Author) decides that. . . .

(Author) urges that. . . .

(Author) recalls that. . . .

All of these verbs can take variant forms like those shown for *states* and *says*.

SPECIAL CASES

More than One Author

What do you do if your source has more than one author? Just name them all. For example:

```
As Eunice S. Grier and Atlee E. Shidler state, . . .

According to Marilyn Merritt, Ailie Cleghorn, and
Jared O. Abagi, . . .
```

If you instead put the authors' names in parentheses, give the last names: (Grier and Shidler 66), (Merritt, Cleghorn, and Abagi 232). Be sure that the names appear in the same order both in citing works and in the list of Works Cited. The order is the one in which the names are listed in the work itself.

But suppose a work has more than two or three authors: perhaps half a dozen or more, as in the case of some scientific studies where many researchers have contributed to the published findings. In such a case, the limit is common sense. While it is important to acknowledge one, two, or three authors in the statement about your source, more than three will weight it down too much. With four or more authors you would list only the "primary" author—the one whose name appears first on the title page and first in the entry for the work in your list of Works Cited—and add the Latin phrase "et al.," an abbreviation meaning "and others."

For example, when the authors are listed as Randolph Quirk, Sidney Greenbaum, Geoffrey Leech, and Jan Svartvik, you could write

```
     According to Randolph Quirk et al., . . .
```
   or
```
     . . . (Quirk et al. 144).
```

More than One Work by One Author

You may very well find an expert in your field who has written more than one work you would like to cite. That's no problem for the list of Works Cited; you simply write a separate listing for each separate source, even if the author is the same. Alphabetize the listings as usual, first by author's name, then according to the titles of the works. After the first of the listings, replace the author's name with three hyphens typed together. (Use the hyphens only when the two names are exactly the same. If the next work in the list is by the previous author and another person, for example, use both names, not hyphens.)

When your list has more than one work by the same author, how do you cite them? To make clear which source you are using, you must tell your reader the title of the work as well as the author's name. The title can be part of your statement about the source or it can go in parentheses just before the page number. A short form of the title will do, as long as it is different from the author's other titles. For example:

```
     In Just Looking, John Updike states . . . (27).

     Updike is not overly sympathetic to writers who
  write of the agony of writing ("Books" 106-107).

                    Works Cited
  Updike, John.  "Books: Writer-Consciousness."  The New
       Yorker 65 (25 December 1989): 103-108.

  ---.  Just Looking: Essays on Art.  New York: Alfred A.
       Knopf, 1989.
```

Author Citing Author

And what do you do when one author cites another? You simply say so to your reader and go on with your usual citation of the source you used. For example:

```
     Euell Gibbons quotes several lines from Robert
Frost's poem "Blueberries" as evidence that blueberries
thrive after a forest fire (41).

                      Works Cited
Gibbons, Euell.   Stalking the Wild Asparagus.   New York:
     David McKay Company, 1962.
```

The (41) in parentheses refers to page 41 in Gibbons's book, which is where the lines from Frost's poem are found. Another method is to add the phrase "quoted in" to parenthetical citation of the source.

```
     Robert Frost's poem "Blueberries" gives evidence
that blueberries thrive after a forest fire (quoted in
Gibbons 41).
```

EXERCISE 10.1—CITING WORKS

For each of the following, write one or more sentences that cite the work and then a Works Cited listing. The statements about each source do not need to be changed, except to include citation.

1. A character in this book doubts that any book can really examine a person's life. The book is the novel *American Appetites* by Joyce Carol Oates. It was published by E. P. Dutton in New York in 1989, and the character's thought is on page 146.

2. In the *MLA Handbook for Writers of Research Papers*, third edition, it says that each citation of a source in the text of the paper must lead the reader to one specific entry in the list of Works Cited. The citation does that by including whatever comes first in the entry. This is on page 156. The authors are Joseph Gibaldi and Walter S. Achtert, the publisher is The Modern Language Association of America in New York, and the year is 1988.

3. Judith Thurman writes that teenage Anne Frank (author of "The Diary of Anne Frank"), hiding from the Nazis, was ready for love both from boys and from readers. This is on page 120. Her article, "Books: Not Even a Nice Girl," appeared in *The New Yorker*, Volume 65, December 18, 1989, starting on page 116 and ending on page 120.

4. Three of the terms and names that E. D. Hirsch, Jr. thinks every literate American should know are "Berlin, Irving," "Berlin," and "Berlin wall." These are in a list on page 157 of his book *Cultural Literacy: What Every American Needs to Know*. It was published in Boston by Houghton Mifflin Company in 1987. (Hirsch chooses not to capitalize the second word of "Berlin wall," though most authors do. If you use his exact words, putting them in quotation marks, you should follow his style of capitalization.)

5. In its January 1990 issue, Volume 55, No. 1, page 8, *Consumer Reports* says that cars with fuel-injected engines need detergents in their gasoline. No author is indicated for the article, entitled "Which Gasoline for Your Car?" and extending from page 8 through page 10.

∇

CHAPTER ELEVEN

FULL DOCUMENTATION

▽

As appropriate, use special forms and abbreviations in listing sources according to MLA style. As an alternative, use the author–year APA style.

(Chapter 9 gave the principles and three basic forms for listing Works Cited. Details of APA style are given in Appendix III. If you have mastered the principles of documentation, proceed to write about the sources, Chapters 12–16.)

▽

The system of citing and listing used in this book follows the most widely accepted patterns for documenting research. It is modeled in particular on the pattern established by the Modern Language Association of America for scholarship in literature and language, but it is also close to that of the American Psychological Association for research in the social sciences.

Full details of MLA style and APA style are more complex than given here. In fact, each of them requires an entire book. The book from which we extract our principles is

Gibaldi, Joseph and Walter S. Achtert. MLA Handbook for Writers of Research Papers. 3rd edition. New York: Modern Language Association of America, 1988.

MLA style is also presented in this handbook for scholars:

Achtert, Walter S. and Joseph Gibaldi. The MLA Style Manual. New York: Modern Language Association of America, 1985.

If you are writing a work of advanced scholarship—a thesis or dissertation, or an article to submit for publication in a scholarly journal, or a scholarly book—you will want to get *The MLA Style Manual* and follow its exact prescriptions. For most research purposes, however, Chapters 9 and 10 of this book will suffice. They give the basic principles behind MLA style and the basic forms. Applied intelligently to the sources you encounter, these principles and forms will produce citations and listings that are fully compatible with advanced MLA style.

If you understand and apply the principles of Chapters 9 and 10, this chapter will not be necessary. It does, however, offer help with special cases, and it explains some of the characteristics of advanced MLA and APA style. (For specifics on APA style, see the end of the chapter and Appendix III.)

SPECIAL CASES OF MLA STYLE

Anthologies

A work in an anthology or collection is treated according to the pattern for an article in a book. For example:

```
Chaucer, Geoffrey.  "The Nun's Priest's Tale."  The
    Norton Anthology of English Literature.  5th
    edition.  Edited by M. H. Abrams.  New York: W. W.
    Norton & Company, 1986.  1: 209-223.
```

Introduction, Foreword, or Preface

If a work is a collection of pieces by various authors, the introduction is treated as an article in a book. For example:

```
Abrams, M. H.  "Preface to the Fifth Edition."  The
    Norton Anthology of English Literature.  Fifth
    edition.  Edited by M. H. Abrams.  New York: W. W.
    Norton & Company, 1986.  1: xxx-xxxvii.
```

Newspaper Articles

An article in a newspaper is treated like any article in a periodical—with minor adjustments for the distinctive features of newspapers. Many newspapers appear in different editions for different circulation areas and times of day, so you will want to include information on the edition if that is given: Late Edition, City Edition, and so forth. Volume number will usually be found on the front-page nameplate.

Page numbers can be a particular problem with newspapers because many newspapers come in more than one section and each section starts with page 1. To direct your reader to the right page of a newspaper, therefore, you must include section number as well as page number at the end of your Works Cited—just as you include volume number along with page number for an article in an encyclopedia or other multi-volume work. If the different sections are labeled by letters of the alphabet A, B, C, and so forth, simply put the letter of the alphabet in front of the page number. If sections are designated by Roman numerals, change Roman to regular Arabic and use with the abbreviation Sec.: Page 1 of Section IV should be listed as Sec. 4: 1, for example.

Here are sample entries for *The New York Times*. The article by Clines begins on the front page, page 1 of section A, and continues on page 15 of section B.

```
Clines, Francis X.  "Tribute to Vietnam Dead: Words, a
     Wall."  New York Times Late Edition 132 (11 November
     1982): A1, B15.

Lin, Maya Ying.  "The Vietnam Memorial."  Letter to the
     editor.  New York Times Late Edition 130 (14 July
     1981): A24.

"The Vietnam Names."  Editorial.  New York Times Late
     Edition 132 (11 November 1982): A30.
```

Editorials, Reviews, or Letters to the Editor

Special types of articles in newspapers, magazines, or journals are labeled as such after the title. Two of the above newspaper listings include labels of this sort. Here is another example:

```
Schickel, Richard.  "Of Time and the River: Coming to
     Terms with Bravery and Tomfoolery."  Review of the
     film Driving Miss Daisy.  Time 134 (18 December
     1989): 91.
```

Government Documents

Government publications do not look exactly like ordinary books and periodicals. Sometimes they have titles that take up a whole page, as in Figure 11-1. At other times they may have no title page at all, just a cover. They are produced by committees and departments—but are those the authors or the publishers, or both? And books are often given an exact month and date as well as year of publication. Or they may have two different dates: one for the submission of a report, another for the date of publication.

Nevertheless, Chapter 9's principles generally apply just as well to government documents as to other kinds of publications. Since government documents are often hard to locate, be generous in including extra information. Document numbers, committee names, and meeting dates all are helpful in a Works Cited listing.

Here is a possible listing for the publication in Figure 11-1:

```
Hunger in America: Hearings before the Subcommittee on
     Nutrition and Investigations of the Committee on
     Agriculture, Nutrition, and Forestry, United States
```

S. Hrg. 100-710

HUNGER IN AMERICA

HEARINGS

BEFORE THE

SUBCOMMITTEE ON
NUTRITION AND INVESTIGATIONS

OF THE

COMMITTEE ON AGRICULTURE, NUTRITION, AND FORESTRY UNITED STATES SENATE

AND THE

COMMITTEE ON AGRICULTURE, NUTRITION, AND FORESTRY UNITED STATES SENATE

ONE HUNDREDTH CONGRESS

SECOND SESSION

ON

HUNGER AND RELATED NUTRITIONAL ISSUES

———

JANUARY 30, 1988—CEDAR RAPIDS, IA
MARCH 1, 1988—WASHINGTON, DC
MARCH 28, 1988—LUTHERAN PLACE MEMORIAL CHURCH,
WASHINGTON, DC

———

Printed for the use of the
Committee on Agriculture, Nutrition, and Forestry

U.S. GOVERNMENT PRINTING OFFICE

85-267   WASHINGTON : 1989

———

For sale by the Superintendent of Documents, Congressional Sales Office
U.S. Government Printing Office, Washington, DC 20402

Figure 11-1

```
Senate, and the Committee on Agriculture, Nutrition,
and Forestry, United States Senate.  Washington, DC:
U.S. Government Printing Office, 1988.  100th
Congress, 2nd Session on Hunger and Related
Nutritional Issues.  Hearings January 30, March 1,
and March 28, 1988.  Senate Hearing 100-710.
```

Another example is a publication without a title page whose cover reads, in its entirety:

United States Department of State
Report to Congress on
Voting Practices in the
United Nations
Submitted Pursuant to
Public Law 100-461
and
Public Law 98-164
April 20, 1989

The only other publication information is this notice in small print inside the back cover:

DEPARTMENT OF STATE PUBLICATION 9710
Bureau of International Organizations Affairs
Released April 1989

Putting together this information according to our book format, we can offer a Works Cited listing like this:

```
United States Department of State.  Report to Congress on
     Voting Practices in the United Nations: Submitted
     Pursuant to Public Law 100-461 and Public Law 98-
     164.  Washington, DC:  United States Department of
     State, 20 April 1989.  Department of State
     Publication 9710, Bureau of International
     Organizations Affairs.
```

Whether to list the title first, as in *Hunger in America*, or the government agency (as author) first, as in the *Report to Congress*, depends on the researcher's judgment: what is the most convenient and logical way of referring to the publication? The simple title *Hunger in America* stands out and suggests giving it precedence over the lengthy name of the subcommittee and committee, while the title *Report to Congress* has so generic a beginning that it may be preferable to start the Works Cited listing with the name of the specific agency.

Sometimes government documents provide their own suggested bibliographic listings on the back of the title page. By all means use them, whenever possible.

Expert help is available in citing and listing government documents. Ask your reference librarian for this excellent book:

Garner, Diane L. and Diane H. Smith. *The Complete Guide to Citing Government Documents*: *A Manual for Writers & Librarians*. Bethesda, MD: Congressional Information Service, Inc., 1984. For the Government Documents Round Table, American Library Association.

Reference Works

Chapter 6 gave examples of citations for encyclopedias. The Works Cited entry for them and other reference works with alphabetical entries is the same as that of an article in a book. For example:

```
"Cue."  The Oxford English Dictionary.  Prepared by J. A.
    Simpson and E. S. C. Weiner.  2nd edition.  Oxford:
    The Clarendon Press, 1989.  4:110.

Cullinane, James J.  "Washington Monument."  The World
    Book Encyclopedia.  Chicago: World Book, Inc., 1990.
    21: 110-111.
```

Translations

The name of a translator is handled like that of an editor, but with the words "Translated by" instead of "Edited by." Here is an example of a translation of three poems (all of them anonymous, so no author is listed):

```
Sir Gawain and the Green Knight, Pearl, and Sir Orfeo.
    Translated by J. R. R. Tolkien.  Boston: Houghton
    Mifflin Company, 1975.
```

The Bible and Shakespeare

The basic principle of citing works, as explained in Chapter 10, is to lead the reader to the proper entry in the list of Works Cited. The citation also tells the reader the exact page of the source that provides the information. Certain works are available in so many different editions that it is preferable to cite them not by page but by standard division—book, chapter, verse; act, scene, line.

The Bible and the works of Shakespeare are well known enough that it is permissible to cite them by naming one of those parts rather than the whole. It is presumed that your reader knows you are dealing with the Bible when you name a book of the Bible, and with one of Shakespeare's works when you name that. For further information, the reader can then turn to Bible or Shakespeare in the list of Works Cited.

Citing the Bible means naming the book of the Bible, chapter, and verse, the latter two separated by a colon. Listing the Bible requires an entry that begins with the word *Bible* so that the reader may find it under the expected heading in the alphabetical list of Works Cited. Following that introductory word give complete publication information, using the standard form for a book. Do not name an author unless your version happens to state the author's name on the title page.

It was formerly sufficient to offer the abbreviated entry "Bible" (meaning King James Version) or "Bible. Revised Standard Version" in the list of Works Cited, when those two were the customary choices. Now that many different versions of the Bible are widely available, it is important to let your reader know the full details of the version you used, including edition and date, as in the case of the recently-published revised Revised Standard Version.

Sacred writings, including the Bible, the Koran, and the Talmud, do *not* have their titles underlined.

A reference to the Bible goes like this:

```
    Creation of the different languages of the world is
said to have occurred when the tower of Babel was built
(Genesis 11: 1-9).
```

Works Cited

(Possible versions: List just the one you cited)

```
Bible.   The Holy Bible: Authorized (King James) Version.
     Philadelphia: National Bible Press, no date.

Bible.   The Holy Bible: Revised Standard Version.
     Cleveland: World Publishing Company, 1962.

Bible.   The New Oxford Annotated Bible with the
     Apocrypha.   Revised Standard Version.   Edited by
     Herbert G. May and Bruce M. Metzger.   New York:
     Oxford University Press, 1977.
```

For references to Shakespeare, the citation is to act, scene, and line of the play, rather than to a page.

```
    King Lear's despair at the death of his daughter
Cordelia is measured by his repetition of "Never" five
times (5.3.310).
```

Works Cited

```
Shakespeare, William.   The Tragedy of King Lear.   Edited
     by Russell Fraser.   New York: New American Library,
     1987.
```

Unpublished Documents

```
Shade, John.   Letter to Vladimir Nabokov.   10 June 1958.
     Charles Kinbote Collection.   Wordsmith University,
     Wye, New York.

Stauder, Gretchen.   "What Is Gaudy?"   Unpublished essay,
     1988.
```

Other Media

The section on "Fitting the Categories" in Chapter 9 tells what forms to use for unconventional sources. The principle remains the same: Decide which of the three basic forms best suits the source, and adapt that to the item you are citing. Here are some examples:

Article in Computer Database

Hess, E. "A Tale of Two Memorials." Art in America 71 (April 1983): 120-127. Dialog file 56, item 156574.

Computer Software

Microsoft Works: Integrated Productivity Software. Version 2.00a. Productivity Software, Inc., 1989. Macintosh system.

Film

Gone with the Wind. Directed by Victor Fleming. Selznick International, 1939.

Interview by the Researcher

Lurie, Alison. Personal interview. 4 April 1989.

Lecture

Decker, Philip. Lecture. Drama 317, Contemporary Drama. MacMurray College. Jacksonville, Illinois, 11 February 1991.

Performance of a Play

Happy End. Book and lyrics by Bertolt Brecht. Music by Kurt Weill. Book and lyrics adapted by Michael Feingold. Directed by Linda Brovsky. Court Theatre, Chicago. 3 March 1989.

Radio or Television Program

Extension 720. Host Milton Rosenberg. WGN Radio, Chicago. 13 December 1989.

A Tale of Two Cities, Part 4. Dramatized by Arthur Hopcraft. Directed by Philippe Monnier. Masterpiece Theatre. PBS. KETC, St. Louis. 10 December 1989.

Recording

Allen, Thomas. Mozart Arias. Audiotape. EMI Records Limited, 4DS-38043, 1984.

MLA STYLE: ABBREVIATIONS

The chief difference between the style taught here and that of the *MLA Handbook* is in abbreviation. For clarity and to avoid misunderstanding, the examples of this book use full names and words. MLA, on the other hand, advocates abbreviation where possible in parenthetical citation and Works Cited listings. But MLA makes this an option: "In choosing abbreviations, keep your audience in mind. While economy of space is important, clarity is more so. Spell out a term if the abbreviation may puzzle your readers" (Gibaldi and Achtert 203).

Abbreviation is convenient for experts—readers who are familiar with research in a field. Not presuming on expertise, this book avoids abbreviation.

But if you write for an expert audience, it is appropriate to follow MLA style in this respect too and abbreviate the names of months, states, and publishers, as well as words like *edited* or *translated*. The *MLA Handbook* devotes six pages to abbreviations of scholarly terms and two pages to abbreviations for the names of publishers, and it even provides abbreviations for the names of books of the Bible, plays of Shakespeare, and the works of Chaucer. Here are some examples of Works Cited listings from earlier in this chapter using MLA-recommended abbreviation:

```
Schickel, Richard.  "Of Time and the River: Coming to
     Terms with Bravery and Tomfoolery."  Rev. of the
     film Driving Miss Daisy.  Time 134 (18 Dec. 1989):
     91.

Shakespeare, William.  The Tragedy of King Lear.  Ed.
     Russell Fraser.  New York: NAL, 1987.

Sir Gawain and the Green Knight, Pearl, and Sir Orfeo.
     Trans. J. R. R. Tolkien.  Boston: Houghton, 1975.
```

For reference works, the effect of abbreviation is even more drastic. "When citing familiar reference books," says the *MLA Handbook*, "do not give full publication information. For such works, list only the edition (if stated) and the year of publication" (111). Because entries are alphabetically arranged, even page numbers may be omitted. Here are some examples:

```
"Cue."  OED.  2nd ed. 1989.

Cullinane, James J.  "Washington Monument."  World Book.
     1990 ed.
```

APA STYLE

Another widely-used system of parenthetical citation is the author-date system of the American Psychological Association. It is similar to the MLA system used here, the principal difference being that it requires stating the year of publication when citing and listing sources. In APA parenthetical citation, the year of publication comes after the author's last name and before the page number. The list of works cited has the heading References, and it too gives prominence to the year, which comes right after the author's name.

Here is an example from the start of this chapter, revised to follow APA style:

```
     T. L. Clark states that very few of the terms for
cheating in gambling have been recorded in historical
dictionaries (1986, 6).
```

```
                     References
Clark, T. L.  (1986).  Cheating terms in cards and dice.
    American Speech, 61, 3-32.
```

If an author has published more than one work in a year, the entries are labeled (1986a), (1986b), and so on.

For further details, see Appendix III.

EXERCISE 11.1—LIST OF WORKS CITED

For each of the following, write an appropriate listing. Put the six entries in an alphabetical list of Works Cited.

1. The Introduction to *The World of Mathematics*, published in four volumes by Simon and Schuster in New York in 1956. James R. Newman is the editor and wrote the introduction. The introduction is on pages vii and viii of Volume 1.

2. An article in Volume 2, pages 774–777 of that anthology. It is called Kinetic Theory of Gases, and the author is Daniel Bernoulli.

3. A review in *Law and History Review*, Volume 7, Number 2, Fall 1989, on pages 390 and 391. The review is by David Thomas Konig. It evaluates a book called *The Witch-Hunt in Early Modern Europe* by Brian P. Levack.

4. A letter to the editor of *Fortune* on page 30 of the January 1, 1990 issue, Volume 121, No. 1. The letter is by William Catlette and has the title The Price of Mistrust.

5. An interview you conducted with the governor of your state last month. State the governor's name and choose an exact date.

6. The first letter to the Corinthians, Chapter 13, verse 13, in the Revised Standard Version of the Bible. Use the edition cited earlier in this chapter.

ASSIGNMENT VIII—ABBREVIATION

If your instructor recommends or requires it, use abbreviations in your list of Works Cited. Abbreviate names of months, publishers, books of the Bible, and also words and phrases like Review, Edited by, and Translated by. See the *MLA Handbook*, available in most reference collections, for specific guidance, but the general rule is to abbreviate wherever clarity will not be lost.

∇

PART IV

Writing About Sources

▽

CHAPTER TWELVE

TAKING NOTES: WRITING TO THE POINT

▽

For each source, write an explanation of the evidence it provides to support, oppose, or modify the hypothesis.

For specifics of summarizing, paraphrasing, and quotation, see the next two chapters. For the organization and form of the final paper, see Chapters 17 through 19.

▽

When you read a source, what kind of notes should you take? If you did not have a hypothesis, that question would be difficult to answer. A source might have a great variety of material to annotate that might be interesting. But since you have a hypothesis, the answer is easy: Take notes on what is relevant to the hypothesis. What is relevant will be interesting, because it will relate to the point by supporting, opposing, or modifying it.

The heart of the research is the thinking process that relates source to hypothesis. Accordingly, what you write about a source should focus on this thinking. Your writing, which develops into the sentences and paragraphs that make up the body of your research paper, should explain what the source has to say in regard to your hypothesis.

The ingredients of a research paper are, on the one hand, a hypothesis, and on the other hand, relevant sources. Your writing makes the connection between the two ingredients.

You, and not your sources, have to make the connection, because your sources do not know what your hypothesis is. Hence you will generally use your own words, rather than the words of the source; and that is why in this book all the examples so far have been of summary and paraphrase, the use of your own words, rather than direct quotation. The coming chapters will deal with the specific techniques of summary, paraphrase, and quotation. This chapter emphasizes keeping to the point—the hypothesis—as you write about your sources.

How much you have to say about a particular source depends not so much on the length of the source as on its relevance. In a short article you may find several matters to mention; a long book may have only one piece of evidence which you find useful for your hypothesis. Again, you must consider your sources not in isolation but in relation to the hypothesis.

Take as a simple example this hypothesis:

▼ Gary Larson's cartoons offer new perspectives on animal life.

Larson's book *The Prehistory of The Far Side* tells about his career, his sources of ideas, his editors, mistakes he has made, reactions from his readers, and so on, but the connection between source and hypothesis would lead the researcher through all that material to statements like these:

```
    Larson may have gained insights into animals while
working as an investigator for the Humane Society in
Seattle (28).

    To honor Larson for his service in bringing biology to the
attention of the public, Dale H. Clayton of the University of
Chicago named a species of chewing lice for him (170).

                    Works Cited
Larson, Gary.  The Prehistory of The Far Side: A 10th
    Anniversary Exhibit.  Kansas City: Andrews and
    McMeel, 1989.
```

Because this central stage of research requires your full attention, there can be a great temptation to put it off—to simply make a photocopy of the source, for example, or to take content notes without regard to the hypothesis—while postponing your consideration of the relationship between source and hypothesis to some future time. Yielding to that temptation is not only inefficient but hazardous, because it allows you to overlook needed modifications in the hypothesis and to enter blind alleys of research that will not fit any hypothesis.

If, on the other hand, you write a statement explaining the relevance of a source as soon as you read it, by the time you finish research you will find that much of the final paper is already written for you.

EXERCISE 12.1—RELEVANCE TO HYPOTHESIS

This is the beginning of an article in the journal *Humanities*, published by the National Endowment for the Humanities:

> Czeslaw Milosz, the 1980 Nobel laureate in literature, writes in Polish but insists on underscoring his Polish-Lithuanian roots. Born in 1911 in rural Lithuania into a family that has spoken Polish since the sixteenth century, Milosz experienced repeated deracinations. In the nearly eight decades of his life, he has been tossed by events in the ideological vortex of this century. His work reflects a fascinating intellectual and cross-cultural journey.
>
> As a small child, Milosz traveled extensively throughout Russia as far as Siberia. Originally a subject of the tsar, he witnessed the fallout from the Russian revolution and saw Poland and Lithuania regain their independence in 1918. He spent his university years in the multiethnic city of Vilnius, studied art in Paris for a year, and visited Italy and absorbed its art. Having survived the horrors of World War II in Nazi-occupied Warsaw, Milosz briefly tasted life under the Communist regime in Poland and proceeded to experience life in the West, first as a member of the Polish diplomatic corps, and then, after his defection in 1951, as an émigré in France. Nine years later he emigrated to the United States. His affiliation with the Slavic department of the University of California at Berkeley afforded him the opportunity to witness first-hand the campus unrest of the 1960s. From his California home he has observed the subsequent metamorphoses of America and his native Europe.

Write a sentence or two explaining the evidence from those paragraphs that is relevant to this hypothesis:

▼ Czeslaw Milosz can be considered an American writer.

Notice that information relating directly to this hypothesis appears toward the end of the second paragraph. Do not mention material that is not relevant. Cite the source and list it in a Works Cited entry.

The paragraphs are from page 18 of *Humanities*, Volume 11, Number 4, dated July/August 1990. The author is Regina Grol-Prokopczyk.

▽

CHAPTER THIRTEEN

SUMMARY AND PARAPHRASE

▽

Relate the source material to the hypothesis in your own words.

(If you wish to use the exact words of a source, see Chapter 14 on quotation.)

▽

In explaining the relevance of a source to your hypothesis, you will need to make clear what the source has to say. Using your own words, you will either summarize or paraphrase. Most often you will summarize, extracting the essence of the relevant material and condensing what the source has to say into a shorter statement. Sometimes, though, you will want to paraphrase, going into as much detail as the source itself.

And sometimes you will simply want to copy the words of the source, that is, to use quotation. The next chapter will give rules for quotation. But since the purpose of a research paper is to investigate a hypothesis you have devised, it is appropriate for most of the words that explain the relevance of the source to be your own, whether summary or paraphrase.

Again it should be emphasized that, even when you use your own words, any use of a source—any summary or paraphrase, as well as quotation—requires citing the source and listing it in the list of Works Cited.

Summary and paraphrase both require your own words, not the words of the source. Your words means your own words, not just a rearrangement of the source. Here are some examples of passages properly and improperly treated.

Consider this hypothesis:

▼ Richard Nixon lied about the Watergate crisis.

Now consider the relationship of that hypothesis to the following passage from page 324 of the autobiography of former U.S. Senator and Presidential candidate Barry M. Goldwater. (For specifics on the source, see the Works Cited listing below.)

President Nixon lied to his wife, his family, his friends, longtime colleagues in the U.S. Congress, lifetime members of his own political party, the American people, and the world. The lies persisted for more than two years, from at least June 23, 1972, when he personally undertook an active role in covering up the Watergate burglary, to his resignation on August 8, 1974. No lie is intelligent, but his were colossal stupidity because they involved the presidency of the United States.

Summary: Satisfactory

A summary of the paragraph, relating it to the hypothesis, could say:

```
Former Senator Barry M. Goldwater is emphatic in saying
Nixon told lies about his involvement in Watergate (324).
```

Summary: Unsatisfactory

```
Former Senator Barry M. Goldwater says President Nixon
lied to his wife, family, and friends (324).
```

```
Works Cited
Goldwater, Barry M. with Jack Casserly.  Goldwater.  New
    York: St. Martin's Press, 1990.
```

The first summary expresses the gist of the passage in the author's own words. The second picks up too many of the words of the source; it is in fact so much a direct quotation that it needs quotation marks:

```
Senatorial leader Barry M. Goldwater said "President Nixon
lied to his wife, . . . family, [and] friends" (324).
```

As Chapter 14 will explain, the three periods indicate ellipsis, or something left out, and the brackets include words or comments added by the researcher. Failure to provide the quotation marks would count as plagiarism, in fact—what we here call plagiarism type B. (See Chapter 16.)

Those examples were of summaries of the passage. But it contains specific information relevant to the hypothesis too. Instead of summarizing, therefore, the researcher could paraphrase, setting down the full information of the passage but using the writer's own words, as in the following example.

Paraphrase: Satisfactory

```
According to Senatorial leader Barry M. Goldwater, Nixon
told lies over the whole two-year period of the Watergate
scandal (324).  He told lies to everyone: not just to the
public, but to politicians, Republicans as well as
Democrats; to his friends, and to his family, even his
wife.  Those who had served with him in Congress for many
years were not spared the lies (324).
```

Paraphrase: Unsatisfactory

```
    According to Senatorial leader Barry M. Goldwater,
President Nixon lied to everyone, namely his wife, family,
friends, and longtime colleagues in the Senate (324).   He
told lies for more than two years, from June 1972 to
August 1974 when he resigned (324).
```

Again, what is wrong with that passage is that is uses too many words from the source. To avoid plagiarism, it would need frequent and distracting use of quotation marks:

```
    According to Senatorial leader Barry M. Goldwater,
"President Nixon lied to" everyone, namely "his wife, . . .
family, . . . friends, [and] longtime colleagues in the" Senate
(324).   He told lies "for more than two years, from" June
1972 to August 1974 when he resigned (324).
```

How do you avoid the error of using too many words of a source when you are trying to paraphrase or summarize? By taking the time to read over and digest the material of the source before you start writing, and then by putting the page out of sight while you write. When you are through writing, it is not only appropriate but necessary to compare your words with those of the source to see whether you need quotation marks, but while you are writing, do not look at the source.

Here is a second example. This is from an article in a scholarly journal, as described in the Works Cited listing that follows. Suppose the hypothesis is:

▼ An important influence on the thinking of Martin Luther King, Jr., was his father.

A paragraph in the source that can be related to this hypothesis is the following:

> In sum, the most important intellectual influence on King does not appear in "Pilgrimage" and rarely makes more than a cameo appearance in accounts of King's worldview. This person provided King an example of a preacher who was also an activist; he proudly sent King to three universities, connected King with Mays and thus with a large Protestant network, and enthusiastically welcomed King as copastor during the last eight years of King's life, despite the allegedly foreign ideas King had acquired in supposedly alien graduate programs. Had King credited this person—his father—white readers of "Pilgrimage" would hardly have admired King or granted him a philosophical persona. But we should not dismiss Martin Luther King, Sr.

Summary: Satisfactory

```
    Keith D. Miller writes that Martin Luther King, Sr.,
supported his son not only financially but through example,
connections, and an appointment to share the pastorate of his
church (77).
```

Summary: Unsatisfactory

Keith D. Miller writes that Martin Luther King, Sr., provided King an example of a preacher, sent him to college and a large network, and gave him an enthusiastic welcome as copastor for the last eight years of his life (77).

Works Cited

Miller, Keith D. "Composing Martin Luther King, Jr." PMLA 105 (January 1990): 70-82.

The second summary in this case is unsatisfactory not merely because it takes words from the source without using quotation marks, but because in so doing it misreads the source. What it says is not what the source says. "Sent him to college" may not be literally wrong for "sent King to three universities," but it does not suggest the extent of King's education. And King was not sent "to a large network," as if that meant a radio or television network; what the source means is that King's father introduced his son to Benjamin Mays, president of Morehouse College, who in turn introduced him to other Protestant thinkers. Finally, it was the last eight years of the son's life, not the father's, during which they shared a pulpit. Careless reliance on the words of a source can lead to nonsensical explanation.

Paraphrase: Satisfactory

Keith D. Miller argues that even though Martin Luther King, Jr., does not mention his father in the essay on his thinking called "Pilgrimage to Nonviolence," his father had more influence on his son's intellectual development than anyone else (77). Aside from providing a role model and supporting his son throughout his undergraduate and graduate studies, the elder King introduced his son to the president of Morehouse University and thereby to a network of Protestant theologians. Furthermore, the father happily shared the pastorate of his church with the son for eight years, until the son's death (77).

Paraphrase: Unsatisfactory

Keith D. Miller writes that Martin Luther King, Sr., made a cameo appearance in the book called "Pilgrimage" (77). Furthermore, this person was an example of a preacher. He was proud to send King to three colleges and a large Protestant network. Also during the last eight years of his life he welcomed foreign ideas and alien graduate programs because his son was copastor. White readers did not admire King, but they never dismissed his father (77).

This second version is again not only a collection of unacknowledged quotations from the source but a misreading of it. In fact, it is hard to make any sense at all of the second version. The writer probably did not understand the passage and was groping desperately to say something by putting the words of the source in new combinations. That practice usually leads to nonsense. It is why you need to get a basic understanding of your topic (Chapter 6) before you conduct your research.

EXERCISE 13.1—CORRECTING MISREADING

In the unacceptable second paraphrase of the passage on Martin Luther King, Jr., identify and correct each mistaken statement. Put quotation marks around phrases that are the same as in the original passage to show that they were written by the author of the original.

EXERCISE 13.2—SUMMARY AND PARAPHRASE

Take as a hypothesis:

▼ Plastics have become increasingly useful.

For this hypothesis first summarize and then paraphrase the following passage from *National Geographic*, Volume 176, December 1989. Also cite and list the source. The article, "Reshaping Our Lives: Advanced Materials," by Thomas Y. Canby, begins on page 746 and ends on page 781.
From page 767:

> For a new material to succeed, it usually must be able to muscle aside a metal or glass; after all, they got there first. The masters of this have been the synthetic plastics, a family of materials that didn't exist a century ago.

This section of the article continues on page 770:

> In 1907 Belgian immigrant Leo Baekeland invented Bakelite, a hard synthetic substance for making billiard balls and wire insulation. But Baekeland did not completely understand the complex chemistry he exploited.
> That triumph fell to Du Pont chemist Wallace H. Carothers. In the 1930s he combined carbon, hydrogen, nitrogen, and oxygen—the basic ingredients of you and me—into long molecular chains. Neoprene and nylon were the results—the first wholly synthetic materials ever made by a knowing manipulation of molecular structure. They launched the materials revolution that now reshapes our world.

EXERCISE 13.3—SUMMARY AND PARAPHRASE

Take as a hypothesis:

▼ Writing is not a heroic occupation.

For this hypothesis first summarize, then paraphrase the following passage by the writer John Updike in his review, "Books: Writer-Consciousness" in

The New Yorker of December 15, 1989, Volume 65, pages 103 through 108. Also cite and list the source. The passage is on page 106.

A Democracy of honest workmen, it may be, resists the idea that doing one kind of labor deserves more exaltation and excuses more self-indulgence than doing another kind. The shoemaker, for example, doesn't get moony and mock-heroic about pounding out his shapely, intricate product, and doesn't ask to be especially praised for sticking to his last. Yet shoes are more plainly useful than books. We all have chosen, in submission to the passions of childhood and accidents of adulthood, lasts to stick to, and the trade of writer is, with its unstructured hours, opportunities for self-expression, and possible rich rewards, sufficiently attractive so that there are far more applicants than positions available. The lucky few able to see their product into published, distributed, profitable form should be quiet about it, and exaggerate neither the hardships nor the glory of their achievement.

ASSIGNMENT IX—WRITING ABOUT SOURCES

For each relevant source, write one or more sentences paraphrasing or summarizing source material to show how it supports, opposes, or modifies your hypothesis. You may use the worksheets in Appendix II.

$$\triangledown$$

CHAPTER FOURTEEN

QUOTATION

▽

Use quotation marks (" ") for the same words in the same order as in the source, and avoid quotation marks for words that are not the same words in the same order as in the source. Do not overuse quotation. Introduce each quoted passage with your own words.

(If you use your own words rather than the words of the source, see Chapter 13 on summary and paraphrase. Whether or not you use the words of a source, be sure to cite it [Chapter 10].)

▽

One thing has been missing from the previous discussion of using sources: quotation.

That omission was deliberate. To quote is to use the words of a source instead of the researcher's own words. In a sense, this is the opposite of what Chapters 12 and 13 ask, that you explain the relevance of the source material in your own words. If you present a source merely by quoting it, you explain nothing; your reader is left to figure out its relevance. That is not the point of research.

In fact, a research paper does not need any quotation at all. This is in contrast to parenthetical citation and the list of Works Cited, which are always necessary. They are to be used any time you refer to a source, even when you use your own words.

Nevertheless, quotation has its uses—providing you add to it your own explanation of its relevance. You must be sure to introduce the quotation with your own words, and explain the quotation further after you have presented it, if necessary.

Handled this way, quotation from a primary source can have documentary value, stating the precise conditions of a legal agreement or describing a scene in the exact words of a witness. Quotation can be also used when a source happens to speak directly to your point, or when the words of the source are especially striking and well chosen. "We hold these Truths to be self-evident," says the Declaration of Independence, "that all Men are created equal, that they are endowed by their Creator with certain unalienable Rights, that among these are Life, Liberty, and the Pursuit of Happiness." Now suppose a hypothesis stated that

▼ The founders of the United States were advocates of human rights.

With that source and this hypothesis, it would be awkward to insist on paraphrase and say

```
        Jefferson spoke for all the colonies when he wrote in the
Declaration of Independence that a reason for independence was
to make sure of three rights: the right to remain alive, the
right to be free, and the right to fulfill one's desires.
```

Instead, quotation of the Declaration's famous phrase would be in order:

```
        Jefferson spoke for all the colonies when he wrote in the
Declaration of Independence that a reason for independence was
to secure the "unalienable Rights" of "Life, Liberty, and the
Pursuit of Happiness" (1).
```

```
                        Works Cited
A Declaration by the Representatives of the United States of
        America, in General Congress Assembled. Philadelphia, 4
        July 1776.
```

Occasional use of quotation can add variety and spice to the research paper. Quotation is best treated as seasoning, to be added with a light touch, not as a main course. When you do quote, quote sparingly. The presumption is that you will use your own words unless you have a good reason to borrow the words of a source.

The rule for quotation is simple:

• Use quotation marks (" ") for the same words in the same order as in the source, and avoid quotation marks for words that are not the same words in the same order as in the source.

It follows that any time you copy two or more words from the source in the same order as they appear in the source, you must put those words in quotation marks. (This means two or more words that do not routinely go together, so phrases like *this nation* or names like *the Mississippi River* and *Joyce Carol Oates* by themselves will not need quotation marks.) Conversely, any time you use words that are different from the words of the source, you must *not* use quotation marks.

Or to use an analogy: Quotation is like taking a photograph. When you use quotation marks, you tell your reader you are photographing the source— giving the exact words, spellings, capitalization, and punctuation marks of the source in the exact order that they appear in the source, no more and no less. (Notice the copying of unusual capital letters and the spelling of *unalienable* in the quotation from the Declaration of Independence, for example.)

However, you can indicate that you have left out one or more words or sentences by putting an ellipsis in every place where you have left something out. An ellipsis is three periods with space before and after each one (. . .).

And you can indicate you have put in words or comments of your own by putting those added words or comments in square brackets [ ].

Let us take a few examples.

Hamlin's illustrated survey of American architecture, noted in Chapter 9, provides evaluations of the Washington and Lincoln monuments in language that relates them to the hypothesis about American ideals. Here is a paragraph from his page 225:

THE WASHINGTON MONUMENT,
WASHINGTON

But there are other monuments in which sculpture plays no part at all. The most famous of these is the Washington monument by Robert Mills, begun 1848, completed 1884 by General T. L. Casey. Its effect lies entirely in the delicate tapering of the great mass of the obelisk — pure geometric form attaining beauty by virtue of its perfect proportion. In the very fact of its total lack of ornament there is a commanding dignity, a mighty strength, eminently fitted for its purpose.

As in Chapter 13, we could summarize or paraphrase here rather than use quotation:

> Talbot Faulkner Hamlin, in his 1926 survey <u>The American Spirit in Architecture</u>, observes that the simplicity and plainness of the Washington Monument lend it power and authority (225).

Works Cited

> Hamlin, Talbot Faulkner. <u>The American Spirit in Architecture</u>. New Haven: Yale University Press, 1926.

(You will notice that in citing the source, the sentence gives the title and year of the source in addition to the author's name and the page number. Title and year are not necessary, but they can be useful under certain circumstances. In this case, the title suggests that the emphasis of the book is on the spirit rather than the technical details of architecture. And the year indicates that this is a view from the 1920s rather than from the present day.)

But there is another way to make use of the source. Hamlin's own words relate eloquently to the hypothesis of the paper. If we make proper use of quotation marks, it would be perfectly appropriate to use some of those words. We could write a sentence like this:

Talbot Faulkner Hamlin, in his 1926 survey <u>The American Spirit in Architecture</u>, observes that the "total lack of ornament" of the Washington Monument lends it "a commanding dignity, a mighty strength" (225).

Comparing the sentence that uses quotation marks with the original paragraph from Hamlin's book, notice that the words *total lack of ornament* are the same words in the same order in both sentences—so the sentence citing the source puts those words in quotation marks. Notice, likewise, that the words *a commanding dignity, a mighty strength* are the same words in the same order, so they too get quotation marks.

But notice that between the two quotations is material that does not appear in the original. Where the source joins the two quotations with *there is*, our sentence uses *of the Washington Monument lends it*. The two phrases do not match, so the quotation marks have to end and begin again, rather than continuing through the mismatched words.

Notice also that the sentence using the quotations does not begin with quotation. To make sure quotations tie in with the hypothesis you are discussing, you must *begin every sentence with your own words*, even if you wish to quote from the source.

And notice, finally, that quotation as we describe it here does not mean looking for words that are already in quotation marks in a source. We will deal with that special case later. Rather, quotation means adding *your* quotation marks to something borrowed, word for word, from a source.

Let us turn to another example from Hamlin, this time his page 231.

THE FIGURE OF LINCOLN WITHIN

In the interior the austerity of the Doric gives way to the pure grace of the Ionic; and in the middle, on his simple throne, sits Lincoln, calm, reposeful, noble. Queerly enough the old Greek forms from hundreds of years ago seem perfectly in harmony, seem almost perfectly to express the strength and the dignity and the humanity that were Lincoln's. Therein lies part of the reason for the success of the whole.

Making use of quotation, we can relate source to hypothesis as follows:

Abraham Lincoln is the central figure in his monument. Though he led the United States during its fiercest internal struggle, neither his statue nor his pose suggest defiance or military might. In Hamlin's words, Lincoln is depicted as "calm, reposeful, noble" (231). Hamlin adds, "the old Greek forms from hundreds of years ago . . . seem almost perfectly to express the strength and the dignity and the humanity that were Lincoln's" (231).

This example provides further illustration of these rules:

- Words in " " are the same as the words of the source; words not in " " are not the same as the words of the source.

- Using " " is like taking a photograph: you keep the same words in the same order, along with the original spelling, capitalization, and punctuation.

- Sentences do not begin with quoted words but are introduced by the researcher's own words.

- Using " " does not mean looking in the source for words that already have " " around them. Instead, it means adding " " to words taken from a source.

The example also illustrates one additional point:

- Use an ellipsis (. . .) to show that something has been left out of a quotation. In the example above, the ellipsis replaces *seem perfectly in harmony*, four words plus a comma. The ellipsis does not tell how much has been left out; it is the same whether you leave out just one word or a hundred. But if you leave out anything, be sure to put an ellipsis in its place, or you will not be copying exactly.

The next example (Figure 14-1) is from a *Facts on File* report. Using quotation, we can write as follows:

```
    The Vietnam Veterans Memorial was at first criticized
because, in the words of a Facts on File report, it "did not
adequately reflect the heroism of U.S. troops in the war"
("Vietnam War Memorial Becomes National Monument" 867).
```

Vietnam War Memorial Becomes National Monument

New Statue Completes Tribute. The Vietnam Veterans Memorial formally became a national monument Nov. 11 (Veterans' Day) at the conclusion of three days of ceremonies in the Washington, D.C. area. [See 1982, p. 863C1]

The ceremonies honored Vietnam veterans under the umbrella title "Salute II." They began Nov. 9, with the unveiling of a bronze statue sculpted by Frederick Hart, *Three Servicemen.*

The statue stood on the Washington Mall, about 80 feet (25 meters) from the sunken "V"-shaped black granite walls that made up the original monument. The walls were inscribed with the names of 58,022 Americans either killed or missing in action in Southeast Asia.

The monument's organizers in 1982 had agreed to add a statue in response to criticism that the walls alone did not adequately reflect the heroism of U.S. troops in the war.

Three Servicemen depicted in realistic detail a trio of young, war-weary soldiers standing together and facing the granite walls. Each figure was seven feet (two meters) tall. One had white racial features, another, black. The third figure displayed a mixture of ethnic characteristics.

The tribute continued Nov. 10, with a solemn candlelight vigil at the monument.

Source: Copyright © 1984 by Facts on File, Inc. Reprinted with permission of Facts on File, Inc., New York, NY.

Figure 14-1

To reflect this heroism, a statue of three soldiers was
added in 1984. Whether or not these soldiers are heroic
may be open to question. They are of heroic size, each
being "seven feet . . . tall," but <u>Facts on File</u>
describes them as "war-weary" (867).

Works Cited

"Vietnam War Memorial Becomes National Monument." <u>Facts on</u>
        <u>File</u> 44 (23 November 1984): 867.

This example shows how even short phrases need quotation marks. If you
have even two consecutive words (not counting words that routinely go
together) from the source in the same order in your sentence, you must put
them inside quotation marks. And so we have *seven feet . . . tall*, with the
ellipsis showing that the parenthetical *(two meters)* was left out.

Even a single word, if it is a distinctive one representing the style or
outlook of a source, calls for quotation marks. In this case *war-weary*, the
distinctive term used in the article to characterize the statue of the
soldiers, needs to be indicated as coming from the source.

As a final example, let us look at the complication of dealing with
quotation marks already in a source (Figure 14-2). This is from a *New York
Times* interview with Maya Ying Lin, designer of the Vietnam Veterans
Memorial. The following sentences could be written in regard to the hypothesis
about monuments reflecting American ideals:

The architect of the Vietnam Veterans Memorial told <u>The</u>
<u>New York Times</u> that she had been too young to consider the
Vietnam war a "'great issue'" (Ayres B5). While she
personally hated "'all war,'" she said that the V of the
monument's shape "'doesn't have anything to do with
"Vietnam" or "victory" or "veterans"'" (B5).

At the urging of their professor,
Andy Burr, Miss Lin and her class-
mates decided to enter the compe-
tition. In the end, however, only she
and the professor actually submitted
entries.

Miss Lin says she made her
memorial V-shaped and burrowed it
slightly into the ground, up to about 10
feet at the apex, to draw passers-by.
"The V-shape doesn't have anything to
do with 'Vietnam' or 'victory' or
'veterans,'" she explained. "I hate war,
all war. But Vietnam was something I
only remember as a child. There's no
particular great issue about it for me."

Once drawn into the memorial, the
visitor will be confronted, left and right,
by polished black walls of granite, each
200 feet long. On the walls, in
chronological order, will be the names
of the 57,692 Americans who died in
Vietnam.

The memorial is scheduled to be
dedicated on Veterans Day 1982. ∎

Figure 14-2

```
                          Works Cited
    Ayres, B. Drummond, Jr.   "Maya Ying Lin: A Yale Senior, a
        Vietnam Memorial and a Few Ironies." The New York Times
        130 (29 June 1981): B5.
```

When you find quotations in a source you are citing, you simply add your own quotation marks around the material you take from the source. You change the double quotation marks of the source (") to single quotation marks (') but otherwise keep them where you found them. If the source itself uses single quotation marks within double ones, as this example does, these too get changed to preserve the contrast of one layer of quotation within another.

Notice also the placement of periods and commas at the end of quotations. A period or comma goes inside closing quotation marks, even if there are several of them and even if the period or comma is not part of the original quotation. But if a parenthetical reference comes at the end of the quotation, the period or comma is postponed until the end of the parenthesis.

BLOCK QUOTATIONS

Our examples of quotation so far have all been short, no longer than a single sentence at most. That is the most appropriate way to use quotation—sparingly. But on a rare occasion it may be necessary to quote something longer, as much as a couple of sentences.

If a quotation amounts to more than four typed lines, it is too long to tuck into your paragraph. You have to set it in a separate block, without added quotation marks, and indented ten spaces from the left. If the original contains quotation marks, keep them in your block. Double space, as usual.

Remember to lead in to the quotation with your own words. For a block quote, your words will usually end with a colon (:) just before the block begins. Put the page number in parentheses at the end of the block. Here is one example of a paragraph from an article on the Vietnam Veterans Memorial and a block quotation from it:

> But, as I have said, the overwhelming sentiment felt at the Memorial's dedication was patriotic, and so therapeutic. Even as the speakers expressed fears of entangling foreign alliances, most everyone seemed to feel that America is still like a ray of the sun in a somber world. In this way the ceremony and the Memorial once again served the cause of union. Complete strangers embraced each other. I repeatedly heard people saying "welcome home" to veterans, as though they had not been back all the while.

```
        A scholar who was present at the dedication of the Vietnam
    Veterans Memorial reports:

                        But, as I have said, the overwhelming sentiment
                    felt at the Memorial's dedication [on 13 November
                    1982] was patriotic, and so therapeutic. . . .  In
                    this way the ceremony and the Memorial once again
```

served the cause of union. Complete strangers
embraced each other. I repeatedly heard people
saying "welcome home" to veterans, as though they
had not been back all the while. (Griswold 714)

Works Cited

Griswold, Charles L. "The Vietnam Veterans Memorial and
    the Washington Mall: Philosophical Thoughts on
    Political Iconography." Critical Inquiry 12 (Summer
    1986): 688-719.

VERSE QUOTATION

The rules for quoting poetry are the same as for quoting prose, except that you indicate to the reader where the lines of poetry end. If you have only one, two, or three lines of poetry to quote, treat them like the other short quotations we have discussed earlier. That is, put the quoted lines in quotation marks and include them in your own sentences. Use a slant line with space before and after (/) to show where the poetry breaks from one line to the next. For example:

The chief character of Richard Wilbur's "Finished Man"
achieves greatness through forgetfulness of the past. Wilbur
sums up the man's attitude with "If the dead die, if he can but
forget, / If money talks, he may be perfect yet" (42).

Works Cited

Wilbur, Richard. "A Finished Man." The New Yorker 61 (4 March
    1985): 42.

If you need to quote more than three lines of verse, make it a block quote, indenting ten spaces. As before, put the page number in parentheses at the end of the block. Double space, as usual. Keep the lines of verse the same as the original. (Remember, quotation is like a photograph.) For example:

The "Finished Man" of whom Wilbur writes is an impressive
benefactor of his college:

        Thus he can walk today with heart at ease
        Through the old quad, escorted by trustees,
        To dedicate the monumental gym
        A grateful college means to name for him. (42)*

To summarize this chapter on quotation: Quotation marks tell when you are using the exact words of a source. Use them, then, whenever you use the same words in the same order as in your source; avoid them when you use different words, or when you change the order. Once you have finished writing sentences about a

---

*Reprinted by permission; © 1985 Richard Wilbur. Originally from *The New Yorker*.

source, check your sentences against the sentences of the source to see whether and where you need to put quotation marks. But quotation cannot take the place of your own explanation of how a source relates to your hypothesis.

EXERCISE 14.1—USING QUOTATION

Take as a hypothesis:

▼ Writing is not a heroic occupation.

For this hypothesis write sentences incorporating quotation from the John Updike review used in the exercise at the end of Chapter 13. Remember to cite author and page, and to lead in to quotation with your own words.

EXERCISE 14.2—USING QUOTATION

Take as a hypothesis:

▼ Americans are superstitious.

For the hypothesis write sentences incorporating quotation from the following article. It appeared in the *St. Louis Sun* newspaper (Vol. 1, No. 99) for January 1, 1990, on page 24. The article, by Tom Siegfried, is titled "Carl Sagan: The Scientist vs. the Soothsayers." If you use Sagan's own quoted words, be sure to use quotation marks within quotation marks. Write a Works Cited listing too.

> ITHACA, N.Y. — Astrology, says Dr. Carl Sagan, is a very bad sign for science.
>
> In particular, the world's best-known astronomer finds astrology to be a sign of inadequate attention to science in the nation's mass media.
>
> "Every newspaper in America has a daily astrology column, with one or two exceptions," he said recently in a speech to science writers at Cornell University. "Virtually no newspaper in America, as far as I know, has a daily science column."
>
> Efforts to get newspapers to include a disclaimer with horoscope columns, stating that astrology has no scientific basis and should be read strictly for entertainment, have been largely unsuccessful. Newspapers continue to provide astrologically derived advice on a daily basis. . . .*

$$\triangledown$$

---

*Reprinted with permission of *The Dallas Morning News*.

CHAPTER FIFTEEN

PLAGIARISM TYPE A— FAILURE TO CITE AND LIST

▽

Every time you make use of a source, cite it and make sure it appears in the list of Works Cited. Do this even if you do not use the words of the source.

(For specifics of citation, see Chapter 10. For specifics of Works Cited listings, see Chapters 9 and 11. The mechanics of quotation are discussed in Chapter 14.)

▽

Although it involves the work of others, a research paper is essentially your own thinking on a point, thinking that is informed and supported by the sources you have found. For clarity, as well as to give credit where credit is due, it is essential to show where your work leaves off and the work of others begins. Failure to do this is a serious academic malfeasance known as plagiarism.

Plagiarism is making someone else's work appear to be your own. In its simplest form, it is outright fraud. You know that you must write your own paper, not copy a friend's.

But what is simple enough to avoid in an ordinary essay is more complicated in a research paper. Even while you conscientiously avoid copying what your neighbor has written, you can accidentally commit two different kinds of plagiarism while writing a research paper. One kind has to do with citing works, and we will discuss it here as Plagiarism Type A. The other kind, Plagiarism Type B, will have our attention in the next chapter.

Plagiarism Type A is *failure to credit author and source for information taken from that source.* If you do not cite and list a source, the reader assumes that what you write comes from your own knowledge and experience. The 500-word research proposal at the end of Chapter 4, for example, cites no sources because it comes from the general background knowledge and experience of the author, who at that point has not yet started research.

As soon as you start looking at sources, however, the picture changes. The sentences that relate the information in a source to your hypothesis must cite the source by the means explained in Chapters 9 and 10. That is, your sentences must name the author and a specific page or pages, and in turn you must have a Works Cited listing for each author and work.

Please note, again, that citing and listing have nothing to do with whether you use quotation or not. Whether you state the information entirely in your own words, or quote the actual words of the source, you must always cite and list the source.

COMMON KNOWLEDGE

An exemption is made for "common knowledge." You do not need to cite and list a source for something any halfway educated person would know or that can be found in any reference work—that *1984* is an anti-totalitarian novel by George Orwell, that Jessica Tandy is the oldest Oscar winner for Best Actress, that Julius Caesar reformed the calendar, that the French Revolution followed the American one.

But use this exception sparingly. Common knowledge, after all, should not be the subject of a research paper; your paper should seek support that is beyond common knowledge.

Whether something might be considered "common knowledge" or not, if you had to look it up, cite and list your source. And if you happen to know something that is specialized information, find a source anyhow and cite and list it, so that you will have authority not just of your own assertion.

For a summary list of serious errors in documentation, including citing and listing, see Appendix IV.

EXERCISE 15.1—CITATION

The paragraph below relates to the hypothesis

▼ Charles Dickens suffered hardship as a child.

To the paragraph add the citation and a Works Cited listing so that it will avoid Plagiarism Type A. The paragraph summarizes material on page 38 of *Dickens: A Biography* by Fred Kaplan, published in New York by William Morrow & Company in 1988.

When Dickens was only twelve years old he was put to work in a factory managed by a friend of the family. The factory made shoe polish, and Dickens' job was to paste the labels on pots of polish ready for distribution. At first he was kept apart from the lower-class boys who did other work in the factory, but soon he was moved downstairs to be with them.

▽

CHAPTER SIXTEEN

PLAGIARISM TYPE B— FAILURE TO ACKNOWLEDGE QUOTATION

▽

Use quotation marks for the same words in the same order as in the source, and avoid quotation marks for different words or different order.

(For specifics of quotation, see Chapter 14.)

▽

Chapter 15 warned about Plagiarism Type A, failure to cite a source of information. Inaccurate use of quotation can lead to an equally serious fault, which we will call Plagiarism Type B. If you use the words of others but do not put them in quotation marks (or block quotation), you have plagiarized— because the reader assumes that words not in quotation marks are your own words.

It can happen by accident. While trying to write a statement in your own words, you may be so influenced by what you have been reading that you accidentally copy two or more words from the source without adding quotation marks. That is just an oversight, but it is also Plagiarism Type B.

This is how to guard against it: Unless you intend direct quotation, first read the source and then put it out of sight, so that as you write you will not be influenced by the exact words of the source. When you have finished writing your sentences, open the source again and check what you have written against the original, word for word. If you find in your sentences two or more words from the original in the same order as in the original, put quotation marks around the copied words. (As Chapter 14 explains, this means two or more words not routinely associated—so phrases like *the Canterbury Tales, on the other hand,* and full names do not need quotation marks.)

Plagiarism Type B is also one reason why making a photocopy of each page you cite is important. As the next chapter will explain, the sentences you write about sources become the raw material for your research paper. You will often want to modify these sentences when you incorporate them into the paragraphs of the paper. In that process, as the wording changes, the quotation may also be changed.

So you must check the finished version of your paper, not just the original sentences, against the sources to make sure you have used quotation marks properly and avoided Plagiarism Type B. If you have made copies of the cited pages, this final check will be easy and convenient. To make it even more convenient, be sure you write author and page number on the copy and highlight the particular passages you cite or quote.

In applying quotation marks (or block quotation) to words from a source, be careful not to apply them too widely. Just as quotation marks are necessary to indicate that words come from the source, so it is necessary to avoid quotation marks when words are not the same and in the same order as in the source. If the words are almost the same, you may use ellipses (. . .) and square brackets [ ] as explained in Chapter 14 to indicate changed material.

For a summary list of serious errors in documentation, including quotation, see Appendix IV.

EXERCISE 16.1—QUOTATION

Take as a hypothesis:

▼ Different languages have different systems of meaning.

Take as a source in support of the hypothesis:

Paragraph from book

The larger question of synonymy and bilingual lexicography is a profound one beyond the scope of this book. For example, two words in English may be near synonyms, such as *brute* and *beast*, but their respective translations into another language may be completely unrelated. Contrariwise, two words in English that are semantically unrelated may correspond in translation to two near synonyms in another language.

Now consider the following paragraph relating the source to the hypothesis. The paragraph makes a clear connection, so there is no problem with the meaning. But it uses words from the source without acknowledgment. Add quotation marks so that it will avoid Plagiarism Type B.

Sentences about the passage

In his book on lexicography, Sidney Landau offers an example of how two words may be completely unrelated in one language, while their translations may be near synonyms in another language (110). The words he uses as examples are <u>brute</u> and <u>beast,</u> which in English are near synonyms, but translated into other languages may have nothing to do with each other (110).

Works Cited

Landau, Sidney I. <u>Dictionaries: The Art and Craft of Lexicography</u>. Cambridge, England: Cambridge University Press, 1989.

▽

PART V

The Final Paper

▽

CHAPTER SEVENTEEN

THE FINAL POINT

▽

Convert your hypothesis to a final thesis statement, limiting and adjusting it as necessary to fit the evidence provided by the sources.

(For organization and outline of the paper, see Chapter 18. Specifics of form are given in Chapter 19.)

▽

With the notes you have on hand, the paper is already half written. Those notes, explaining the evidence offered by sources in regard to your hypothesis, are ready to be incorporated into the body of the research paper, where they will do the same thing for your final thesis. That final thesis will develop from your research hypothesis, modified as necessary to take into account the evidence you have found.

NARROWING THE HYPOTHESIS

If you have searched diligently, you may find yourself with more material than you can incorporate into your paper. In that case, you have two choices. One is to select from your sources only the best, the most relevant and significant. The other is to narrow your final thesis statement, taking for the whole paper what began as just a part. Consider, for example, this hypothesis:

▼ The monuments of Washington, D.C. reflect American ideals.

If an overabundance of evidence is on hand to support it, the hypothesis might be developed into a much more focused thesis:

▼ The Vietnam Veterans Memorial reflects ideals of equality and the worth of the individual.

Even if you do not have too much material, the evidence you have gathered may still show that your initial hypothesis needs narrowing. For example, if you start with this hypothesis:

▼ Television watching weakens the academic performance of high school students.

you may find evidence that results in a more specific thesis such as this one:

▼ Watching more than ten hours of television a week weakens the academic performance of above-average high school students.

Here are some other examples.

Original hypothesis:

▼ Lowering tax rates raises tax revenue.

Narrowed final thesis:

▼ Lowering personal income tax to a maximum of 40 percent increases tax revenue from those with the highest income.

Original hypothesis:

▼ Seat belts save lives.

Narrowed final thesis:

▼ Seat belts reduce injuries in 80 percent of auto accidents and increase injuries in 10 percent.

So to determine the thesis you must return to the hypothesis and reconsider it. Does the evidence you have gathered support it completely or does it need modifying?

Probably it needs modifying. You now know more than when you began, and you must let this new knowledge be reflected in your final thesis. The thesis statement is a one-sentence summary of everything your paper says. Everything in the paper relates to the thesis, so the thesis must take account of everything you now know. It probably will have to change at least a little from its initial formulation.

ACCOUNTING FOR OBJECTIONS

In particular, the hypothesis may need to be modified to account for evidence against it.

Any hypothesis worthy of research is capable of being challenged. That is why the assignment for the 500-word research proposal (Chapter 4) required a statement of possible objections, as well as your reply to them. In the final analysis, possible objections still need mentioning, and they still need your replies.

Maybe the objections are based on misinformation and misunderstanding; maybe they are accurate, but just not as impressive as the information you have found in support of the hypothesis. Whatever the situation, you must deal with it in your paper. And the more significant the objections, the more they should be reflected in the final thesis.

Take, for example, the hypothesis that

▼ Communism is inefficient.

Research on this hypothesis will certainly find arguments to the contrary by Communists saying their system is more efficient, although such arguments are not often heard nowadays. Taking account of these objections to the hypothesis, you may end with a thesis like this:

▼ After decades of arguing that their system is the most efficient, even Communists in the Soviet Union now agree that it is disastrously inefficient.

You may not be entirely happy with the evidence your sources have provided. They may have changed your view of a situation more than you like. But if you wish your research paper to make sense, no matter how much you prefer your original hypothesis, you must be ready to change it to accord with the facts.

Just as you decided on a hypothesis before starting research, so it is important to decide on the final thesis statement before proceeding to write the final research paper. Take time at this point to do it.

ASSIGNMENT X—THESIS STATEMENT

Reviewing the evidence of your sources, convert your hypothesis to a final thesis statement for your research paper. Let the thesis statement be a one-sentence summary of all you are going to say; limit the thesis according to the limits you have found in your research, and acknowledge significant opposing evidence.

▽

CHAPTER EIGHTEEN

OUTLINE AND ABSTRACT

▽

Begin the paper with the thesis; follow it with the supporting evidence, and end by replying to objections.

(On determining the thesis, see Chapter 17. For the form of the paper, see Chapter 19.

▽

Having determined the final thesis statement, you are now ready to arrange the evidence that supports it. This evidence appears in your paper as explanation of why the thesis deserves support, using the statements you have written about the relevant material in your sources.

The statements add up quickly. You can see this by simple arithmetic. If you look at the examples of writing about sources in the preceding chapters, you will see that they average 40 words or more—and these examples were made deliberately brief. If you have a dozen sources for your paper and use each one, on the average, two times for 50 words each, you will have half of a 2500-word paper already written in your notes.

How are these notes to be arranged? In a logical pattern that supports your point.

ORGANIZING THE PAPER

There are two widely used patterns for organizing writing: narrative and expository. The narrative pattern tells a story, usually in chronological order, beginning at the beginning and coming to a resolution at the end. The expository pattern, on the other hand, makes its point at the beginning and then supports it with subpoints arranged in order of importance. We see examples of these two patterns every day. The narrative pattern is that of novels, movies, and television adventure programs or situation comedies. The expository pattern is that of newspaper, radio, or television news; the main point comes first, followed by details.

A research paper is expository. It announces a point—the hypothesis, now transformed into the final thesis—and then states the support for the point. The most obvious way to organize your paper, then, is in the expository manner, something like this:

I. (Introduction and) thesis.

II. Subpoints supporting the thesis, starting with the strongest supporting evidence.

III. Strongest objections to the thesis.

IV. Reply to the objections.

V. Summary and conclusion.

Aside from being convenient, the advantage of this organization is that it gives your paper a strong beginning and a strong ending. Your strongest evidence is at the beginning; your handling of objections to the thesis is at the end.

How do you handle objections? You look for the strongest case that might be made against your thesis, and present it briefly. They you respond directly to the objections, explaining why they do not overturn your thesis. Maybe the opposing arguments are simply wrong; maybe there is evidence on the other side, but it does no more than put a limit on the thesis, or else it is weak in comparison with the evidence on your side.

Although the research paper always begins with the thesis, the nature of the evidence for the thesis sometimes permits other kinds of organization. If the evidence is in the nature of a story, you may be able to organize it in narrative form. Suppose, for example, that your thesis is

▼ The power of television made possible the overthrow of Nicolae Ceausescu's dictatorship in Romania.

With this thesis, it might be natural to present evidence of that influence chronologically, from the public rally where the dictator was defied to the day of his judgment and execution. Remember, though, that the intent of a research paper is to make and support a point; telling a story can be a means to that end, but it is not the end in itself.

Chronological order is also appropriate with a thesis that contrasts two different times, such as the following:

▼ Carbon dioxide emissions have warmed the earth in the past hundred years.

▼ Women's fashions have become less confining during the twentieth century.

If you have not encountered too many surprises since you began thinking about your hypothesis, you may find the 500-word research proposal written for the assignment in Chapter 4 useful as a framework for the final paper. Its subpoints can become the subpoints of the research paper; you simply omit details that came from your own speculation about the hypothesis and replace them with specifics you have gathered from your sources. As necessary, adjust the subpoints (as well as the thesis) to reflect what you have found in your sources.

Once again, if you have conscientiously written statements explaining each source, you will be pleasantly surprised to see that your research paper is already half written. Insert transitional words and phrases to make sure one idea leads smoothly and clearly to the next. Add a brief introduction connecting your thesis to larger issues, and a conclusion doing the same. Those are all the necessary ingredients for a research paper.

OUTLINE

The arrangement you choose for the evidence that supports your thesis may be expressed in an outline. An outline may take a number of shapes, but it always begins with your thesis statement. Then it expresses your major subpoints and, depending on the desired detail, minor points as well. The thesis statement is always a sentence, but the rest of the outline may be either complete sentences or a list of topics. A typical outline will have one summary sentence or topic heading for each use you plan to make of a source, arranged under a few major subheadings.

For your own purposes an outline can be as simple as the arrangement of your worksheets or note cards in the order you have chosen. A more formal outline typically uses Roman numerals for main points, followed by letters of the alphabet and Arabic numbers for lesser points:

I.

    A.

        1.

            a.

            b.

        2.

    B.

II.

It is conventional in such an outline to require a II if you have a I, a B if you have an A, and so on.

If the outline is to be useful, this is the time to prepare it—after determining the final thesis but before writing the paper. It is then a map for the directions the paper will take. Just as you sometimes deviate from the mapped route when making a journey, so it is to be expected that the actual paper may differ somewhat from the outline. An outline that is included with the final paper will then be corrected so that it agrees with the actual details of that paper.

ABSTRACT

An abstract is a highly condensed version of an article or book, giving the thesis and subpoints or principal supporting evidence. You will have encountered abstracts in the abstracting indexes of the library's reference collection (Chapters 6 and 7). With the finished paper (or an outline) at hand, preparing an abstract of your paper is easy. Just begin with your thesis statement and add the three or four most important subpoints from the rest of your research paper. Put these sentences into a single short paragraph—no longer than 100 words—and type it below the title of the paper with the label "Abstract." Because it summarizes the paper, the abstract is best written when the paper is completed and the final points are determined. Accordingly, the assignment to write an abstract comes with the assignment for the final research paper in the next chapter.

Here is an abstract for a paper on the monuments of Washington, D.C. Note that, no matter what form the outline may take, the abstract uses complete sentences in a single paragraph.

```
                    One from Many:

        The Monuments of Washington, D.C.



                        Abstract

        The four monuments in the center of Washington, D.C.
    celebrate neither victory nor glory but democratic
    ideals:  the unity of diverse individuals and the worth
    of each individual.  Grandeur attended the original plans
    for the Washington Monument and divisiveness halted its
    construction for twenty years, but it emerged as an
    unadorned obelisk celebrating unity in diversity.  The
    memorials for Jefferson and Lincoln likewise emphasize
    individual dignity and national unity.  And the recent
    Vietnam Memorial, with its plain marble wall naming the
    fallen beside a statue of three ordinary soldiers, brings
    dignity and unity to the memory of a divisive war.
```

ASSIGNMENT XI—OUTLINE

Write an outline for your research paper. Begin with the thesis statement, then list the major subpoints, either as topics or as sentences, and indicate the chief information you intend to include under each heading. Make clear where you will present and deal with any objections to your thesis. Use formal labeling with Roman numerals, letters, and Arabic numerals if your instructor requires it; otherwise numbering is not necessary.

▽

CHAPTER NINETEEN

FINAL FORM

▽

Follow standard form; inform your reader of the dates of your material; limit introduction and conclusion each to 5 percent of your paper.

(On the thesis, see Chapter 17. On organization of the paper, see Chapter 18.)

▽

With the thesis statement determined and the supporting evidence arranged, it is time to write the final research paper. This chapter explains the form and discusses some final details of the content.

FORM OF THE PAPER

Margins
   Indent an inch (at least) all around.

Paragraphs
   Indent five spaces.

Typing or printing
   Double-space everything, including titles, block quotes, and Works Cited.

Title page
   There is no title page in strict MLA style, only a heading on the first page, double-spaced at the left margin, that gives your name and course information. But your instructor may want you to have a separate title page, centered and double-spaced, with title at the top, author in the middle, and course information at the bottom.

Outline (if required)
   If there is no title page, the outline is on a separate page or pages with a heading on the first page, double-spaced at the left margin, that gives your

name and course information. If there is a title page, the outline goes on a separate page or pages immediately following the title page.

Abstract (if required)

If there is no title page, the abstract goes on the first page of your paper below the heading and the title but before the beginning of your text. Indent it an extra half inch on the left. If you have a separate title page, the abstract goes on a separate unnumbered page, immediately after the title page and outline and immediately before the first page of the paper itself.

First page

If there is no title page, give your name and course information on the first page, double-spaced at the left margin. Follow that with the title, the abstract (if any), and the start of your text. If you have a separate title page, simply repeat the title at the top of your first page and begin your text.

Page numbers

Starting with the first page of the text, put your last name and the page number half an inch from the top right margin of each page.

Citing works

As Chapter 10 has explained, every time you use a source you cite author (or title, if no author is given) and page (in parentheses), and the citation leads the reader to the right place in the alphabetical list of Works Cited.

Quoting sources

As Chapter 14 states, use direct quotation sparingly—explain the relevance of source material in your own words, not the words of the source. When you do want to quote a source, introduce it with your own words. Do not begin a sentence with quotation.

Endnotes

Occasionally you may wish to discuss the quality of the sources you are using or to comment on some matter that is not directly related to your thesis. You may do so in an endnote. A raised numeral at the end of a sentence corresponds to the same raised numeral in a list of endnotes on a separate page at the end of your paper. Do not use endnotes for citing or listing works, however; that is done in your text and the list of Works Cited.

List of Works Cited

The list begins on a separate page after the end of your text and after the endnotes (if any). Entries are in alphabetical order according to the first words of each entry (ignoring *A, An, The*). The listing has the reverse indentation from the rest of the paper: The first line of each entry is not indented; all other lines are indented five spaces. Reverse indentation makes the first word of each entry stand out so that the reader can quickly find that key word in alphabetical order when turning to the list from a citation in the text.

List of Works Consulted (if required)

Only those sources which you actually cite—whose authors you name in the text of your paper—belong in the list of Works Cited. That is why the word *Cited* is in its name. For your working bibliography you will probably have consulted other sources which you decided not to use. To show the range of your research, you may be asked to name these sources in a list of Works Consulted starting on a separate page after the list of Works Cited. Style and format are exactly the same as for the list of Works Cited.

THE PLAIN STYLE

A research paper does not have to dazzle with its language; it can let the facts speak for themselves. Grand eloquence is not important. In most cases, a plain down-to-earth style suits the research paper better than fancy writing; the plain style suggests that the writer is concerned to get at the truth rather than to achieve fancy effects.

A plain style, however, is not always easy to achieve. There is a natural inclination to want to use big words to go with big ideas. To combat that inclination, read the discussion of the plain style in the final chapter of the most-admired book about writing:

Strunk, William, Jr., and E. B. White. *The Elements of Style.* 3rd edition. New York: Macmillan, 1979.

But the needed style is mostly a matter of common sense. The purpose of a research paper, after all, is to communicate ideas, not to show off vocabulary, and communication calls for the clearest, most direct expression possible. Try to explain so clearly that the reader will be sure to understand your points.

SAY WHEN

When you put together your sentences into a research paper, you are creating something new. It makes use of the information provided by others, but it is your own thesis with your own unique blend of sources.

And because it is a new arrangement, unfamiliar to your reader, you need to provide guideposts for that reader. Above all, whenever you make use of a source, it is helpful to say *when:* when the source was published, when the information presented in the source was gathered, when an event took place. Inform your reader how recent the source is—whether it is something published in the last few months, or the last year or so, or at some earlier time. Even more important is informing your reader of the dates of the material in your sources. If a source says air travel was the safest form of public transportation *last year*, and the source was published in 1984, be careful to say *1983* rather than *last year* in a sentence that presents this information. If a 1972 source says Japan *now* has the world's third-largest economy, don't assume that is still the case for the *now* of your paper. Check the latest figures, or at least say, *"In 1972* Japan had the world's third-largest economy."

Putting in dates is the single most useful addition to help your reader understand the context of your source material. Also useful, though, are indications of the type of publication and the intended audience: a scholarly study, a general-interest book or magazine, a consumer guide, a laboratory experiment or field investigation, the leading scholarly book in the field. The examples given in previous chapters here have frequently added more than the required minimum for the purpose of giving the reader a sense of the sort of source it is. Similarly, it is useful to inform your reader *who* the author of a source may be—one who has a certain scholarly reputation, perhaps, or who shows a certain bias.

INTRODUCTION AND CONCLUSION

Of course a research paper has an introduction and a conclusion. But they should not grow out of proportion. Perhaps no more than 5 percent of the paper should be used for introduction and 5 percent for conclusion. By this rule, if your research paper is 2500 words long, you can allow 125 words for introduction and 125 words for conclusion. Include your thesis statement in the introductory 125 words. It goes best at the end of your introductory paragraph.

Like the rest of the paper, the introduction and conclusion should relate to the point. They are not mere formalities, nor are they merely repetitions of the thesis. Instead, they relate your particular thesis to larger concerns. At the beginning, the introduction can explain why your particular thesis is worthy of attention. At the end, the conclusion can explain what consequences follow from the thesis you have demonstrated, what is likely to happen in the future, or what action should be taken. This is the place for the "should" statement that Chapter 4 cautioned against in the body of your paper. If the thesis states that solar box cookers are effective, for example, the conclusion can declare that grants to teach about solar box cookers *should* be awarded to Third World countries.

It should be noted that an introduction is not the same as an abstract. The introduction (which is the first paragraph of the paper itself) connects your thesis to larger concerns. The abstract, in contrast, is a plain, direct summary of the paper, starting with the thesis statement.

WRITING THE PAPER

So there you have it—a research paper with title page (optional), outline (optional), abstract (optional), introduction, body, conclusion, endnotes (optional), and list of Works Cited. And most important of all—a research paper that is not merely a collection of random remarks from odd sources, but one that presents in-depth information from a variety of respected sources in support of a clearly stated thesis, and that acknowledges and properly responds to challenges to that thesis. You have mastered a body of knowledge, reached a conclusion about it, and reported that conclusion so others can understand and be enlightened by it.

As you give yourself the congratulations that are due, please keep in mind that you have learned these skills not because they are a mysterious ritual devised by professors and librarians, but because they will be useful to you in any future activity where you need to find out more than you already know. You will have discovered that even a modest college library holds a wealth of information on almost any topic; and you now know how to find that information and use it to test an idea (a hypothesis) about that topic. May you apply this skill towards solving the problems confronting our troubled world as it hurtles toward the end of the twentieth century.

Sample pages of a research paper follow this summary assignment.

ASSIGNMENT XII—RESEARCH PAPER

Write a research paper of about 2500 words (ten double-spaced typed pages) plus a title page, an outline, an abstract (see Chapter 18), and a list of Works Cited (see Chapter 9).

Make use of twelve or more in-depth sources of sufficient variety, timeliness, and quality (see Chapter 7).

Present evidence from sources to support your thesis (Chapters 12-13). If you use words from a source, follow the rules for quotation (Chapter 14).

Along with the paper, hand in the cards or worksheets on which you took notes and recorded the Works Cited entries. Also include a photocopy of each cited page, highlighted to show the particular passages you cite in the paper.

Arrange the cards or worksheets with photocopies in the same order as the entries for them in your list of Works Cited. Hand them in with your paper. A folder with pockets is convenient—one pocket to hold the paper, the other to hold the notes with photocopies.

$\triangledown$

American Sign Language as a Language Base
for Hearing-Impaired Children

by
Jamie Kathryn Eshbaugh

Rhetoric 120J, Section 2
Dr. Hanson
23 January 1991

American Sign Language as a Language Base
for Hearing-Impaired Children

Abstract

American Sign Language, or ASL, is an effective
language base for hearing-impaired children. It promotes
conceptual accuracy in the language of these children.
ASL also allows hearing-impaired children to compete with
hearing children academically. As a primary language,
ASL can be utilized in bilingual or English as a Second
Language (ESL) approaches. Finally, this language serves
as a bond between these children, other deaf people, and
the Deaf Community.

Eshbaugh 1

American Sign Language as a Language Base
for Hearing-Impaired Children

For hundreds of years, controversy has raged over the best way to teach language to hearing-impaired children. Strictly oral methods and those leaning more heavily on manual communication have been tried. Manual representations of English have been concocted and the Total Communication philosophy has gained prominence. Despite all this, many hearing-impaired children still demonstrate delayed or inferior English skills. As Pat Spencer Day explains, the reasons for this language delay require knowledge of whether or not the child has "an appropriate communicative base upon which language can be built" (1). Through the years, the native language of the deaf, the heartbeat of their culture, has often been denied its linguistic status and forced underground. Now is the time for this language to attain its rightful stature. American Sign Language, or ASL, is that effective language base for hearing-impaired children.

American Sign Language promotes conceptual accuracy in the language of hearing-impaired children. Harry Markowicz states in his article "Myths about American Sign Language" that the relaying of concepts is the purpose of language (2). If language is so dependent on concepts, then the form of language which best facilitates appropriate meaning would be the most logical for use. In some ways ASL even gives a more clear idea than English. Markowicz gives the example of the sentence "'Bob insulted John and then he hit him'" (6). The reference to "he" is unclear in English, but would be perfectly clear in ASL through the use of pronominalization, placement, and verb directionality (6). An example would be the verb "help," which can mean "May I help you?" when HELP is signed from the signer to the addressee or "Would you help me?" when signed from addressee to signer.

Conceptual accuracy in hearing-impaired children is also shown in how they create new signs to represent objects using ASL. For example, Klima and Bellugi in The Signs of Language describe a three-year-old deaf child who invented signs for 'cinnamon roll,' 'milkshake,' and 'sand crabs' using ASL properties (11). Her sign for 'cinnamon roll' used the inactive cupped hand for the roll and pointer finger to swirl the cinnamon on the roll. Her actions may have been mime-like, but she used handshapes and ways of moving those handshapes that are common in ASL (11). Through this language, hearing-impaired children are encouraged to be creative in presenting their ideas.

Many other systems of coding English into a visual/manual form have been devised, but they are not as mindful of concepts as is ASL. Seeing Essential English (SEE1), Signing Exact English (SEE2), and the Linguistics of Visual English (LOVE) are some of these creations. SEE1 alters ASL rules by using this method: "When the semantic boundaries of an English word differ from those of a sign, those of the sign are extended or narrowed to those of the English word, resulting in one sign for every English word. . ." (Mayberry 408). In SEE1, Mayberry says, if two words have two of the conditions of similar spelling, meaning, or sound, then the same sign is used for both (408).

Stephen P. Quigley and Peter V. Paul in <u>Language and Deafness</u> explain how conceptually inaccurate this is by giving the example of the word "butterfly" (10). BUTTER and FLY would be signed successively. This method, therefore, would not help the mind identify a winged insect. SEE2, as described by Quigley and Paul, is similar to SEE1 except that it treats compound words and complex words differently (10). Because of this, "butterfly" would be signed like a winged creature. LOVE was created to closely correlate to speech rhythm (Quigley and Paul 9). For example, two-syllable words would have signs with two motions (9). LOVE is not conceptual because of the syllabic movements. In contrast, movements and repetitions in ASL have specific meanings. The lack of conceptual accuracy among these three systems makes ASL a better conceptual base for language.

American Sign Language is also an effective language base because it allows hearing-impaired children to compete with hearing children academically. Two ways in which this important point can be shown are through studies comparing the language development of the two groups and through the improving achievements of the hearing-impaired students as compared to the hearing ones. The following studies show that hearing-impaired children can communicate ideas in ASL as well as hearing children can in spoken English. In Grosjean's article, "Psycholinguistics of Sign Language," experiments by Bode (1974) and Jordan (1975) are described (37). Bode's 1974 experiment covered hearing subjects' and deaf subjects' abilities to express and receive messages (Grosjean 37). Bode's conclusions, as described by Grosjean, were that "ASL indeed contains mechanisms for communicating information concerning agent-object-indirect object relationships . . . comparable in effectiveness to those in oral language" (37). Jordan's experiment (1975) involved identification of one correct face picture out of 24 being described (Grosjean 37). The number of errors made by the deaf and hearing subjects (4.83 and 3.96 respectively) were considered to have "a nonsignificant difference" (37). Since expressive, receptive, and descriptive communication are fundamental in education, and since ASL has been shown as effective as spoken language for these areas, hearing-impaired children can compete with hearing children in academics.

Other support for competitive language development in hearing-impaired children reveals parallel language acquisition stages and characteristics. Bonvillian, Nelson, and Charrow in their article "Language and Language-Related Skills in Deaf and Hearing Children" stated that native language acquisition is similar across cultures (232). Because the deaf have their own culture and native language, their acquisition would relate to that of hearing children. In the above article, the research of Schlesinger and Meadow (1972), and Nash (1973) is also used for support on this point (Bonvillian, Nelson, and Charrow 232). Each of these studies used a young deaf subject and found overgeneralizations comparable to those produced by young hearing children (232-233). An overgeneralization by a hearing child might be substitution of the word "doggie" for all animals with four legs. In Schlesinger and Meadow's study, a young deaf girl signed DOG for dogs, different animals, and the "Doggie Diner" restaurant (233). The correlations point similar to language acquisition.

In addition to overgeneralizations, these children also showed two- or three-sign utterances (Bonvillian, Nelson, and Charrow 233). Some examples of these utterances might be MOMMY BOOK (Mommy's book) or ME EAT (I am eating). In the two- or more sign utterances, these children showed a "full range of semantic relations" (233). Hearing children also show tremendous meaning and kinds of statements in two- or three-word sentences.

Finally, the age of relatively good comprehension and mastery is similar to that of hearing children. Deaf children learning ASL, according to a study by Karen van Hoek, Lucinda O'Grady, and Ursula Bellugi, have mastered verb agreement by three years, six months old and have the establishment of

nominals understood by three years old and effectively used by
four years, six months old (9). Hearing children similarly
have a firm command of English before entering elementary
school. The rates of acquisition and levels of attainment of
these hearing-impaired children correlate closely to those of
their hearing peers.

The second way hearing-impaired children can compete with
their hearing peers is through the former's improving
achievement. In the past, hearing-impaired children have done
poorly on standardized tests as compared to hearing children.
In 1972, when Gentile studied the scores of the Stanford
Achievement Test, deaf children scored well in math and
spelling, all right in language, and poorly in science, social
studies, and tests involving meanings of English words (Moores
302). It should be noted that when this study took place
(1972), the focus of education of the deaf was strictly oral
and signs weren't generally encouraged at home or allowed at
school. The low English scores of the tests could be
attributed to inadequate communication and language
comprehension due to this method.

The educational tide has been changing, however. Moores
cites a study by Allen (1986) that used data from 1974 and
1983 on academic achievement of hearing-impaired children
(304). Improvements in arithmetic and reading were found
(304). This improvement correlates with the increased focus
on children's understanding and Total Communication use in the
classroom. Hearing-impaired children are therefore getting
closer to the achievements of hearing children.

Even more promising are the results of studies on deaf
children of deaf parents, who usually have ASL as a native
language. Donald F. Moores in his book Educating the Deaf:
Psychology, Principles, and Practices listed three comparisons
of deaf children of deaf parents and deaf children of hearing
parents which show the superior academic achievements of those
with deaf parents (199). The study by Stuckless and Birch
(1966) indicated that these children were advanced in
"reading, speechreading, and written language" (Moores 199).
The studies of Stevenson (1984) found deaf children of deaf
parents to be better educationally than deaf children of
hearing parents 90% of the time, and the study by Meadow
(1966) found these children years ahead in math, reading, and
overall achievement (Moores 199). Although the superiority of
the deaf children of deaf parents could be due to parental
acceptance of deafness or other factors, the use of ASL

probably has made a substantial contribution to their high
achievement.

Another reason that ASL is an effective language base is
that it can be utilized as a primary language in bilingual or
English as a Second Language (ESL) approaches for teaching
hearing-impaired children. Native users of ASL are like
foreign students in many ways. Often the culture and primary
language of these students are not used in the classroom.
Doreen E. Woodford believes that ignorance of primary language
and proper language development, such as is the case with an
oral-focused education, can lead to poor mental growth and low
self-esteem (39). Woodford also states in her article
"English: First or Second Language? Pidgins, Creoles, and
Identity" that she believes that English language skills could
be better attained by using the first language competently
(42). Her views support the idea that deaf children should
indeed be considered ESL learners and allowed to become
proficient in their native language before attempting English.

American Sign Language-using students also perform like
foreign students in ESL tests. In Richard R. Kretschmer, Jr.,
and Laura W. Kretschmer's chapter called "Language and
Deafness," they discuss the work of Charrow and Fletcher
(1974) with deaf students and the Test of English as a Foreign
Language (TOEFL) (131). Charrow and Fletcher found that the
performance of deaf teenagers with deaf parents (usually
indicating ASL use in the family) was closely tied with that
of hearing students from foreign countries on the TOEFL (131).
This demonstrates how foreign English really is to deaf
children and indicates the possibility that ESL research on
hearing foreigners could be adapted for the hearing-impaired.

In addition, hearing-impaired children can be compared to
others learning English as a second language in the way they
learn and use English. Doreen E. Woodford in her earlier
article, "English: First or Second Language," found incorrect
language usage of deaf pupils similar to that of other ESL
learners because of the consistency of similar linguistic
mistakes throughout the years (171). Other second-language-
learner qualities are also found in hearing-impaired children.
Woodford speaks of "fossilisation" [British spelling], a rigid
nature of language, and "interlanguage," a mixed language used
as a person gains competence in a second language, as
comparable aspects of the two language groups (172). Since
hearing-impaired children have many commonalities with second
language learners, it follows that American Sign Language can

be used as a base language from which to teach English.
Bilingual approaches could therefore be utilized.

 Although few teachers have actually recorded using
English as a Second Language approaches with hearing-impaired
children, these methods have been found effective when used.
Marvin B. Sallop used Manually Coded English and Signed
English with three ASL-proficient students in a class in order
to model proper English syntax (223). In just five weeks
these children began using Signed English signs and therefore
a more English structure in their classroom signing (224).
Sallop attributed the quick learning of the ASL-using children
to their higher language level (224). This successful example
shows that ESL teaching with the deaf is effective. It sets a
precedent for future educational practices of this same type.

 American Sign Language as a language base bonds hearing-
impaired children to other deaf people and to the Deaf
Community. In any community, one of the most vital
characteristics among the people is a common language. Just
as American schoolchildren share ideas and questions in
English, the Deaf Community also has its own language. (The
capitalization of "Deaf Community" appears in response to a
trend in "social and anthropological terms" [Moores 181]).
American Sign Language links the deaf through its wide use and
expression of culture.

 American Sign Language is used by many hearing-impaired
adults. As Hatfield, Caccamise, and Siple state in their work
"Deaf Students' Language Competency: A Bilingual
Perspective," being able to socialize with deaf people in the
Deaf Community requires the acquisition of ASL (847). They
continue by explaining that this language learning occurs
either from birth through deaf parents or through contact with
deaf peers, usually in an educational experience (847). It is
interesting to note that only about 4% of deaf children learn
ASL as a native language from their deaf parents, according to
Moores (28). (Deafness is a low-incidence condition, and it
is rare for deaf people to have deaf offspring). Therefore,
the roles of residential schools for the deaf and those of
deaf peers have high precedence in ASL acquisition.

 Competency in ASL in the Deaf Community is important in
attaining leadership positions as well. A study of 33 elite
deaf persons by Stokoe, Bernard, and Padden indicated that 13
of the 33 had ASL as a native or first language (312). An
example of the importance of ASL socially is the case of one
of the 33 who became deaf just two years before the research

was conducted. He had used sign language for a relatively
short time, but was still accepted as a member of the Deaf
Community's elite (313). His "willingness to use and
communicate in ASL" is cited as a primary reason for his
success (315). Therefore, learning ASL would benefit hearing-
impaired children greatly in the social area of their lives.

Closely related to ASL's role in communication is its
role in culture. Deaf culture is imparted through American
Sign Language. As previously stated, few deaf children have
deaf parents. It logically follows, then, that hearing-
impaired children do not learn of their own culture until
joining a deaf organization or attending a college for the
deaf, such as Gallaudet University. The importance of knowing
one's own culture is referred to by Martha Barnum in her work
"In Support of Bilingual/Bicultural Education for Deaf
Children." Barnum reports J. Cummins' view that success in
bilingual programs is due to pride in that native language and
unique culture (408). Another point made by Cummins is that
ambivalence in culture discourages healthy cognitive and
scholastic growth (Barnum 408). Even the federal government
of the United States states in the Bilingual Education Act
that ". . . a primary means by which a child learns is through
the use of such a child's native language and cultural
heritage . . ." (<u>Toward Equality: Education of the Deaf</u> 41).
Socially, cognitively, and academically, ASL helps prepare
hearing-impaired children to contribute to the Deaf Community
and to the world.

There are various objections that could be expressed
about the use of American Sign Language as a language base for
hearing-impaired children. Strictly aural/oral advocates
could argue that signing by children will hamper speech and
speechreading skills. The objection could also be stated that
hearing parents won't know ASL in order to be able to teach it
to or use it with their children. Manually Coded English
systems could be used as the primary language instead of ASL.

Those are good objections. However, there is an answer
to each one. In Judith Stein Williams' article "Bilingual
Experiences of a Deaf Child," she tells how Meadow's 1968
study showed that sign exposure by deaf children of deaf
parents using ASL led to "'a higher level of intellectual
functioning, social functioning, maturity, independence, and
communicative competence in written, spoken, expressive, and
receptive language'" (184). It is a true problem that hearing
parents of deaf children wouldn't know ASL, but there are many

remedies.   Many community colleges and community centers teach
ASL, and ASL manuals are a possibility, but parent-infant
programs really are important here.   These programs could have
classes, weekend workshops, visiting tutors, and instructional
videotapes which would all prepare the child for later
education at that school or another.   As stated in the section
of this paper on conceptual accuracy, Manually Coded English
systems are not languages and are not generally conceptually
accurate.   In addition, Wilbur (1976) proposed that these
systems leave out "the most important, rich, and unique
features" of English and ASL to produce possibly meaningless
superficial structures (Kretschmer and Kretschmer 132).

   As a final note, American Sign Language and its use in
the education of the hearing-impaired will experience great
change in the years to come.   As states, individuals, and
educators discover the worth and value of this language for
its conceptual accuracy and for its help in academic
achievement, it will become more widespread in programs for
the deaf.   The passing of state laws allowing ASL to be taught
as a foreign language in high schools and the severe ASL
interpreter shortage may lead to better methods of teaching
ASL to hearing people and hearing parents of deaf children.
As American Sign Language gains prominence in education,
hearing-impaired children, the most important asset of the
Deaf Community, will become better educated citizens and
leaders of future generations.

Eshbaugh 9

Works Cited

Barnum, Martha. "In Support of Bilingual/Bicultural Education for Deaf Children." <u>American Annals of the Deaf</u> 129 (November 1984): 404-408.

Bonvillian, John D., Keith E. Nelson, and Veda R. Charrow. "Languages and Language-Related Skills in Deaf and Hearing Children." <u>Sign and Culture: A Reader for Students of American Sign Language</u>. Edited by William C. Stokoe. Silver Spring, Maryland: Linstok Press, 1980. 227-265.

Day, Pat Spencer. "Expression of Communicative Intentions by Young Hearing-Impaired Children." Washington, D.C.: Gallaudet Research Institute, 1985. Unpublished paper presented at the convention of the American Speech-Language-Hearing Association, Washington, D.C., November 23, 1985.

Grosjean, François. "Psycholinguistics of Sign Language." <u>Recent Perspectives on American Sign Language</u>. Edited by Harlan Lane and François Grosjean. Hillsdale, New Jersey: Lawrence Erlbaum Associates, 1980. 33-45.

Hatfield, Nancy, Frank Caccamise, and Patricia Siple. "Deaf Students' Language Competency: A Bilingual Perspective." <u>American Annals of the Deaf</u> 123 (November 1978): 847-851.

Klima, Edward S., and Ursula Bellugi. <u>The Signs of Language</u>. Cambridge, Massachusetts: Harvard University Press, 1979.

Kretschmer, Richard R., Jr., and Laura W. Kretschmer. <u>Language Development and Intervention with the Hearing Impaired</u>. Baltimore, Maryland: University Park Press, 1978.

Markowicz, Harry. "Myths About American Sign Language." <u>Recent Perspectives on American Sign Language</u>. Edited by Harlan Lane and François Grosjean. Hillsdale, New Jersey: Lawrence Erlbaum Associates, 1980. 1-6.

Mayberry, Rachel I. "Manual Communication." <u>Hearing and Deafness</u>. Edited by Hallowell Davis and S. Richard Silverman. 4th edition. New York: Holt, Rinehart and Winston, 1978. 400-417.

Moores, Donald F. <u>Educating the Deaf: Psychology, Principles, and Practices</u>. 3rd edition. Boston: Houghton Mifflin Company, 1987.

Eshbaugh 10

Quigley, Stephen P., and Peter V. Paul. <u>Language and Deafness</u>. San Diego, California: College-Hill Press, 1984.

Sallop, Marvin B. "Pantomime & Gesture to Signed English." <u>Sign and Culture: A Reader for Students of American Sign Language</u>. Edited by William C. Stokoe. Silver Spring, Maryland: Linstok Press, 1980. 217-226.

Stokoe, William, H. Russell Bernard, and Carol Padden. "An Elite Group in Deaf Society." <u>Sign and Culture: A Reader for Students of American Sign Language</u>. Edited by William C. Stokoe. Silver Spring, Maryland: Linstok Press, 1980. 295-317.

<u>Toward Quality: Education of the Deaf</u>. Washington, D.C.: U.S. Government Printing Office, 1988. Report to the President and Congress by the Commission on Education of the Deaf, February 1988.

van Hoek, Karen, Lucinda O'Grady, and Ursula Bellugi. "Morphological Innovation in the Acquisition of American Sign Language." La Jolla, California: Salk Institute for Biological Studies, 1987. Unpublished paper. ERIC document ED 288 374.

Williams, Judith Stein. "Bilingual Experiences of a Deaf Child." <u>Sign and Culture: A Reader for Students of American Sign Language</u>. Edited by William C. Stokoe. Silver Spring, Maryland: Linstok Press, 1980. 181-185.

Woodford, Doreen E. "English: First or Second Language." <u>Journal of the British Association of Teachers of the Deaf</u> 11 (June 1987): 167-172.

---. "English: First or Second Language? Pidgins, Creoles and Identity." <u>Journal of the British Association of Teachers of the Deaf</u> 12 (February 1988): 39-43.

APPENDIX I

THREE BASIC FORMS
FOR THE LIST
OF WORKS CITED

(See Chapter 9 for further explanation)

▽

1. Entire book

Also pamphlet, manuscript, dissertation, unpublished letter, computer printout, lecture, oral interview, painting, musical composition, motion picture, television program, or videotape (page 107); any work that is complete in itself and not part of a larger publication.

Information needed: Entire book

```
Last Name of Author, First Name or Names.  Title of Book.
     Edited by Name of Editor of Book.  Edition of Book.
     Volume(s) used.  City, State of Publication: Name of
     Publishing Company, Year of Publication.
```

Example: Entire book

```
Rosenberg, Bruce A.  Custer and the Epic of Defeat.
     University Park, Pennsylvania:  Pennsylvania State
     University Press, 1974.
```

2. Article in book

Also poem, story, speech in collection, law or court decision, musical piece on tape or disk (page 107); any work that is not in a periodical but is part of a larger publication.

Information needed: Article in book

```
Last Name of Author, First Name or Names.  "Title of
     Article."  Book in Which Article Is Found.  Edited
     by Name of Editor of Book.  Edition of Book.  City,
```

189

```
State of Publication: Name of Publishing Company,
Year of Publication.  Volume number: Pages on which
article is found.
```

Example: Article in book

```
Garcia, Ofelia.  "Bilingualism in the United States:
     Present Attitudes in the Light of Past Policies."
     The English Language Today.  Edited by Sidney
     Greenbaum.  Oxford, England: Pergamon Institute of
     English, 1985.  147-158.
```

3. Article in periodical

Also poem, story, interview, photograph in periodical (page 107); any work that appears in a scholarly journal, magazine, newspaper or other annual volume.

Information needed: Article in periodical

```
Last Name of Author, First Name or Names.  "Title of
     Article."  Title of Periodical Volume number (Day
     Month Year): Pages on which article is found.
```

Example: Article in periodical

```
Miller, Keith D.  "Composing Martin Luther King, Jr."
     PMLA 105 (January 1990): 70-82.
```

APPENDIX II

SOURCE WORKSHEETS

Choose the version of the worksheet that fits the type of source: book, article in book, or article in periodical (see Appendix I and Chapter 9).

Begin reviewing the source with the current version of your hypothesis in mind. There is room to write the hypothesis at the top of the worksheet, or you can write the hypothesis on one worksheet and make photocopies.

Everything you write should relate the source to the hypothesis. Does the source material support the hypothesis, oppose it, or modify it? Say so and explain, giving the details. Be sure to *cite* the source when you use it (see Chapter 10).

These notes—the sentences you write—will then be ready to incorporate into your final paper (see Chapters 18 and 19).

SOURCE WORKSHEET #1—BOOK

Hypothesis _____

_____

_____

    How does the material in this source support (or modify or oppose) the hypothesis?

        _____

_____

_____

_____

_____

_____

_____

_____

_____

_____

_____

_____

_____

_____

Entry for list of **Works Cited** (omit items not available)

```
Last Name of Author, First Name or Names. Title of Book.
     Edited by Name of Editor.  Edition.  Volume(s) used.
     City, State: Publishing Company, Year.
```

_____

    _____

    _____

    _____

SOURCE WORKSHEET #2—ARTICLE IN BOOK

Hypothesis _____

_____

_____

How does the material in this source support (or modify or oppose) the hypothesis?

_____

_____

_____

_____

_____

_____

_____

_____

_____

_____

_____

_____

_____

Entry for list of **Works Cited** (omit items not available)

```
Last Name of Author, First Name or Names.  "Title of
    Article."  Title of Book.  Edited by Name of Editor.
    Edition. City, State: Publishing Company, Year.
    Volume: Pages on which article is found.
```

_____

_____

_____

SOURCE WORKSHEET #3—ARTICLE IN PERIODICAL

Hypothesis _____

_____

_____

How does the material in this source support (or modify or oppose) the hypothesis?

_____

_____

_____

_____

_____

_____

_____

_____

_____

_____

_____

_____

_____

_____

Entry for list of **Works Cited** (omit items not available)

```
Last Name of Author, First Name or Names.  "Title of
     Article."  Name of Periodical Volume number (Day
     Month Year): Pages on which article is found.
```

_____

_____

_____

APPENDIX III

APA STYLE

In the social sciences, research papers generally follow the American Psychological Association's system for citing and listing works. The full-length guide to this system is listed here using the MLA style:

```
Publication Manual of the American Psychological
     Association. 3rd edition. Washington, D.C.: American
     Psychological Association, 1983.
```

The chief difference between this APA style and the MLA style taught elsewhere in this book is emphasis on the year of publication. In APA style, for example, the guide would be listed as:

```
Publication manual of the American Psychological
     Association (3rd edition, 1983). Washington, DC:
     American Psychological Association.
```

LISTING SOURCES
APA STYLE

Here are listings of the three basic types of sources in APA style. Compare these with the forms given for MLA style in Appendix I.

Information needed: Entire book

```
Last Name of Author, First Initial or Initials.  (Year of
     Publication).  Title of book (Edition, Volume[s]
     used).  Edited by Name of Editor of Book.  City,
     State of Publication: Name of Publishing Company.
```

Example: Entire book

```
Rosenberg, B. A.  (1974).  Custer and the epic of defeat.
     University Park, PA: Pennsylvania State University
     Press.
```

Information needed: Article in book

Last Name of Author, First Initial or Initials. (Year of
    Publication). Title of article. In Name of Editor
    (Ed.), <u>Book in which article is found</u> (Edition,
    Volume number: Pages on which article is found).
    Edited by Name of Editor of Book. City, State of
    Publication: Name of Publishing Company.

Example: Article in book

Garcia, O. (1985). Bilingualism in the United States:
    Present attitudes in the light of past policies. In
    S. Greenbaum (Ed.), <u>The English language today</u> (pp.
    147-158). Oxford, England: Pergamon Institute of
    English.

Information needed: Article in periodical

Last Name of Author, First Initial or Initials. (Year,
    Month Day of Publication). Title of article. <u>Title
    of Periodical</u>, <u>Volume number</u>, Pages on which article
    is found.

Example: Article in periodical

Miller, K. D. (1990, January). Composing Martin Luther
    King, Jr. <u>PMLA</u>, <u>105</u>, 70-82.

Citing Sources APA Style

Just as the APA listing of references emphasizes the year of publication, so does the citing of these sources in the text of your paper. The year is inserted between the author's name and the page numbers in parentheses, using punctuation as in these examples:

In the United States, "learned" bilingualism that comes
from learning a second language in school has more favor than
the "natural" bilingualism that comes from learning a second
language at home (Garcia, 1985, pp. 155-160).

Miller (1990, p. 77) writes that Martin Luther King, Sr.,
supported his son not only financially but through example,
connections, and an appointment to share the pastorate of his
church.

DETAILS OF APA STYLE

Use these guidelines when preparing an APA list of references:

1. If an author has published more than one work in a year, the entries are labeled (1986a), (1986b), and so on.

2. Give month and day only with magazines and newspapers, not with journals that have consecutive paging throughout a volume year.

3. If a work has no author, the title moves to the author position before the year of publication.

4. Alphabetize entries first by author, then by date.

5. Initials rather than full first names are generally used for authors.

6. Titles of books and articles do not use capital letters except for the first word and proper names.

7. Titles of articles do not use quotation marks.

SAMPLE CITATIONS AND LIST OF REFERENCES

The following pages show textual citations and the List of Works Cited of the sample paper at the end of Chapter 19 changed to APA style. Notice that instead of the author's last name, a short version of the title appears with the page number.

In the text of the paper, using APA rather than MLA calls for a brisker, more parenthetical style. Authors are introduced by last name only; the year in parentheses always follows. Inside parentheses and in the list of references, & substitutes for *and* in naming authors. Here are some examples:

```
      For example, Klima and Bellugi (1979, p. 11)
describe a three-year-old deaf child who invented signs
for 'cinnamon roll,' 'milkshake,' and 'sand crabs' using
ASL properties.

      SEE2 is similar to SEE1 except that it treats
compound words and complex words differently (Quigley &
Paul, 1984, p. 10).

      Bode's 1974 experiment covered hearing subjects' and
deaf subjects' abilities to express and receive messages
(Grosjean, 1980, p. 37).

      Bonvillian, Nelson, and Charrow (1980, p. 232) state
that native language acquisition is similar across
cultures.

      A study of 33 elite deaf persons indicated that 13
of the 33 had ASL as a native or first language (Stokoe,
Bernard, & Padden, 1980, p. 312).
```

References

Barnum, M.   (1984).   In support of bilingual/bicultural
    education for deaf children.   <u>American annals of the
    deaf</u>, <u>129</u>, 404-408.

Bonvillian, J. D., Nelson, K. E., & Charrow, V. R.
    (1980).   Languages and language-related skills in
    deaf and hearing children.   In William C. Stokoe
    (Ed.), <u>Sign and culture: a reader for students of
    American Sign Language</u> (pp. 227-265).   Silver
    Spring, MD: Linstok Press.

Day, P. S.   (1985, November).   <u>Expression of
    communicative intentions by young hearing-impaired
    children</u>.   Paper presented at the convention of the
    American Speech-Language-Hearing Association,
    Washington, DC.

Grosjean, F.   (1980). Psycholinguistics of sign language.
    In H. Lane & F. Grosjean (Eds.), <u>Recent perspectives
    on American Sign Language</u> (pp. 33-45).   Hillsdale,
    NJ: Lawrence Erlbaum Associates.

Hatfield, N., Caccamise, F., & Siple, P.   (1978).   Deaf
    students' language competency: A bilingual
    perspective.   <u>American annals of the deaf</u>, <u>123</u>, 847-
    851.

Klima, E. S. & Bellugi, U.   (1979).   <u>The signs of
    language</u>.   Cambridge, MA: Harvard University Press.

Kretschmer, R. R., Jr., & Kretschmer, L. W.   (1978).
    <u>Language development and intervention with the
    hearing impaired</u>.   Baltimore, MD: University Park
    Press.

Markowicz, H.   (1980).   Myths about American Sign
    Language.   In H. Lane & F. Grosjean (Eds.), <u>Recent
    perspectives on American Sign Language</u> (pp. 1-6).
    Hillsdale, NJ: Lawrence Erlbaum Associates.

Mayberry, R. I.   (1978).   Manual communication.   In H.
    Davis & S. R. Silverman (Eds.), <u>Hearing and deafness</u>
    (4th edition, pp. 400-417).   New York: Holt,
    Rinehart & Winston.

Moores, Donald F.   (1987).   <u>Educating the deaf:
    psychology, principles, and practices</u> (3rd edition).
    Boston: Houghton Mifflin.

Quigley, S. P. & P. V. Paul.   (1984).   <u>Language and
    deafness</u>.   San Diego, CA: College-Hill Press.

American Sign Language 15

Sallop, M. B. (1980). Pantomime & gesture to Signed English. In W. C. Stokoe (Ed.), <u>Sign and culture: a reader for students of American Sign Language</u> (pp. 217-226). Silver Spring, MD: Linstok Press.

Stokoe, W., Bernard, H. R., & Padden, C. (1980). An elite group in deaf society. In W. C. Stokoe (Ed.), <u>Sign and culture: a reader for students of American sign language</u> (pp. 295-317). Silver Spring, MD: Linstok Press.

<u>Toward quality: Education of the deaf</u>. (1988). (Report to the President and Congress by the Commission on Education of the Deaf.) Washington, DC: U.S. Government Printing Office.

van Hoek, K., O'Grady, L., & Bellugi, U. (1987). <u>Morphological innovation in the acquisition of American Sign Language</u>. La Jolla, CA: Salk Institute for Biological Studies. (ERIC Document Reproduction Service No. ED 288 374)

Williams, J. S. (1980). Bilingual experiences of a deaf child. In W. C. Stokoe (Ed.), <u>Sign and culture: a reader for students of American sign language</u> (pp. 181-185). Silver Spring, MD: Linstok Press.

Woodford, D. E. (1987, June). English: First or second language. <u>Journal of the British Association of Teachers of the Deaf</u>, <u>11</u>, 167-172.

Woodford, D. E. (1988, February). English: First or second language? Pidgins, creoles and identity. <u>Journal of the British Association of Teachers of the Deaf</u>, <u>12</u>, 39-43.

APPENDIX IV

SERIOUS ERRORS IN DOCUMENTATION

(See Chapters 15 and 16)

▽

LISTING

1. **Failure to provide an entry in the List of Works Cited** for every source acknowledged in the text.
2. **Failure to provide full information in the List of Works Cited:** For a book: author, title, city of publication, publisher, year, and other appropriate information such as second edition, editor, volume. For an article in a book: that information plus author, title, and full range of pages for the cited article. For an article in a periodical: author, title, periodical, volume number, exact date of issue, full range of pages, and other appropriate information.
3. **Faulty reference:** wrong information about the work.

CITING: PLAGIARISM TYPE A

4. **Failure to acknowledge a source of information or ideas** by citing author and page in the paragraph where you use the information or ideas.
5. **Failure to acknowledge the source of a direct quotation** by citing author and page in the paragraph where you use the quotation.
6. **Failure to acknowledge a source within a source:** If your source is quoting or taking information from another source, you must make that clear in your text.
7. **Faulty citation:** wrong information about the source.

QUOTATION: PLAGIARISM TYPE B

8. **Misuse of quotation marks:** failure to use quotation marks to indicate words copied from a source, or using quotation marks for words not copied from a source.

9. **Inaccurate quotation:** failure to copy words, punctuation and capitalization exactly when enclosing material in quotation marks.

METHOD OF AVOIDING
SERIOUS ERRORS:

Check every quotation and every citation and listing against a copy of the original source before turning in a paper.

APPENDIX V

SUMMARIES OF ASSIGNMENTS

(Note: These are summaries only. Further explanations and examples are given in the chapters indicated.)

▽

Assignment I—Hypothesis: Following the instructions of Chapter 2, write a possible hypothesis for your research paper. Make sure it is not just a topic, but a sentence that says what the topic is or was, does or did. (More in Chapter 2, page 18.)

Assignment II—500-Word Research Proposal: Write an informal essay of 500 words explaining your views in support of your hypothesis, based not on library research but on what you already know and what you think might be the case. (More in Chapter 4, page 38–39.)

Assignment III—Key Words: After acquainting yourself with the format and method of *Library of Congress Subject Headings*, use it to make a list of key words for your own research hypothesis. Start with the words of the hypothesis and see what related, broader, and narrower terms *LCSH* provides. (More in Chapter 5, page 54.)

Assignment IV—Background for Research: Using the key words you developed in chapter 5 with the help of the *Library of Congress Subject Headings*, and using the encyclopedia's index volume to locate appropriate articles, look in a general encyclopedia for evidence relating to your hypothesis: evidence to support, oppose, or modify it. (More in Chapter 6, page 73.)

Assignment V—Working Bibliography: Locate sources of sufficient quantity, variety, timeliness, and quality that offer material relating to your hypothesis. Compile a working bibliography composed of those that are most promising. If your instructor does not specify the number of sources you must have, use the rule of thumb that about a dozen sources should suffice for a research paper of about 2500 words (8-10 pages). (More in Chapter 7, page 90.)

Alternate Assignment V—Annotated Working Bibliography: In Assignment V, following each Works Cited listing, add a sentence or two in which you summarize the relevance and usefulness of this source to your hypothesis. (More in Chapter 7, page 90.)

Assignment VI (Optional)—Computer Search for Sources: If you have access to a computer database, devise a search strategy for your research hypothesis and try it out on the database. Use the results of the search to modify your strategy as necessary so that it will obtain a dozen sources of appropriate variety, timeliness, and quality. (More in Chapter 8, page 99.)

Assignment VII—Documentation: Whenever you find a source relevant to your thesis, determine which of the three basic forms it fits and write a Works Cited entry for it. Then if you later decide to cite the source in your paper, you will not have to go back for further information. You may use the worksheets in Appendix II. (More in Chapter 9, page 116.)

Assignment VIII (Optional)—Abbreviation: Use abbreviations in your list of Works Cited wherever clarity will not be lost. Abbreviate names of months, publishers, books of the Bible, and also words and phrases like Review, Edited by, and Translated by. (More in Chapter 11, page 134.)

Assignment IX—Writing about Sources: For each relevant source, write one or more sentences paraphrasing or summarizing source material to show how it supports, opposes, or modifies your hypothesis. You may use the worksheets in Appendix II. (More in Chapter 13, page 145.)

Assignment X—Thesis Statement: Reviewing the evidence of your sources, convert your hypothesis to a final thesis statement for your research paper. Let the thesis statement be a one-sentence summary of all you are going to say; limit the thesis according to the limits you have found in your research, and acknowledge significant opposing evidence. (More in Chapter 17, page 165.)

Assignment XI—Outline: Write an outline for your research paper. Begin with the thesis statement, list the major subpoints (either as topics or as sentences) and indicate the chief information you intend to include under each heading. Make clear where you will present and deal with any objections to your thesis. Use formal labeling with Roman numerals, letters, and Arabic numerals if your instructor requires it. (More in Chapter 18, page 170.)

Comprehensive Assignment XII—Research Paper: Write a research paper of about 2500 words (ten double-spaced typed pages) plus a title page, an outline, an abstract, and a list of Works Cited.

Make use of twelve or more in-depth sources of sufficient variety and quality.

Present evidence from sources to support your thesis. If you use words from a source, follow the specific rules for quotation.

Along with the paper, hand in the cards or worksheets on which you took notes and recorded the Works Cited entries. Also include a photocopy of each cited page, highlighted to show the particular passages you cite in the paper.

Arrange the cards or worksheets with photocopies in the same order as the entries for them in your list of Works Cited. Hand them in with your paper. A folder with pockets is convenient—one pocket to hold the paper, the other to hold the notes with photocopies. (More in Chapter 19, page 175.)

INDEX

A 0
B 1
C 2
D 3
E 4
F 5
G 6
H 7
I 8
J 9